Gardens
of the World

Graham, Sandra & Linda Ross

Contents

*To baby Melaleuca, we can't wait to share
these gardens with you as you grow.*

Acknowledgements

We take this opportunity to thank the 23,000 travellers who have accompanied us on more than 400 garden tours during the past 30 years; you have made our garden adventures a pleasure. Thanks to our style guide Robin Powell, editor Carolyn Beaumont and New Holland Publishers. None of these flower-filled adventures could take place without the dedication of the Ross Garden Tours team: Royce Green, Roslyn Willis, Vicky Delatovic, Peter Whitehead, Carolyn Dwyer, Michael McCoy and Libby Cameron. We are immensely grateful to you all.

Happy travels, *The Ross Family*

Introduction

Travelling the globe in search of the world's greatest gardens is our dream come true. Since 1980 we have travelled to far-flung places to find and enjoy thousands of gorgeous gardens. Choosing our favourite gardens was never going to be easy. On what criteria should they be judged: beauty, history, location, plant selection or design? Our quest in search of the world's best gardens took in thousands of magical places we never dreamed existed. We have included gardens from all the major styles, eras and from all continents. Our final selection includes cottage gardens, formal parterres, inspiring public parks, romantic perennial gardens, water gardens, stroll gardens and large parkland estates. Passionate gardeners have created these gardens: royalty, emperors, cardinals, popes, landscape architects, horticulturists and ordinary home gardeners.

This book reflects of our love of gardens, plants, history and knowledge that has accumulated over 30 years. Here we wrap up our favourite gardens from all corners of the globe for you to enjoy at your leisure and give you all the information you need to visit them yourself. We hope you enjoy them.

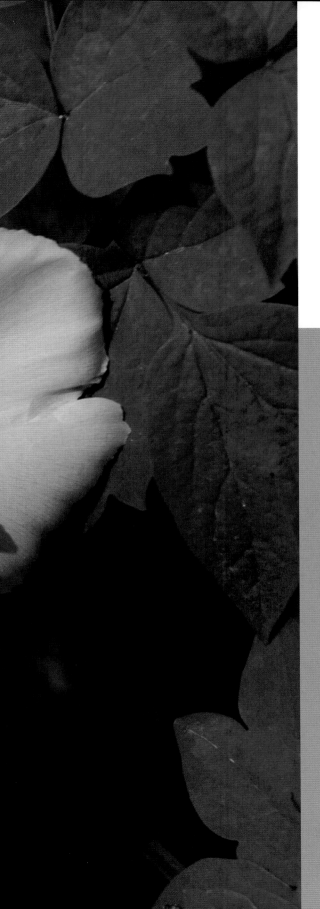

Chapter 1

ASIA

From the tranquil stroll and Zen gardens of Japan, to the bustling living 'attractions' of China, to the tropical exuberance of Indonesia, Asian gardens have fascinated and influenced Western modes of thinking since the days of Marco Polo. These ancient complex cultures are rich in religious symbolism with an Eastern philosophy very different to our own.

Asian gardens are based less on flower displays and more on the holistic sum of the parts. Gardens are designed as a total package, some incorporating the 'borrowed' or distant scenery, with an emphasis on the balance between yin and yang or the feminine (water, foliage) and masculine (pavilions, rocks).

Peony, the 'flower of riches and honour', is the floral emblem of China.

China

Of all the plants grown in gardens around the world, 80 per cent originate in China. China's plants and gardens have fascinated the West since the late 13th century, but it wasn't until the 18th and 19th centuries that Europeans gained access to China's botanical riches.

Throughout China's history, a succession of ruling dynasties, warlords, emperors, wealthy merchants and religious leaders directed and financed the construction of grand gardens. Many were later destroyed by new rulers and cultural influences. The 1978 Open Door Policy saw not only China changed forever but rescued her garden remnants from oblivion.

We have taken tour groups through China every year since 1981 and marvelled at the Herculean efforts of central and provincial governments in restoring gardens to their original glory. Over the past 30 years the Chinese have shown an unswerving belief in the value of their garden heritage and in their beautiful and internationally acclaimed flora that has become popular all over the world. We time our travels for spring (April–May) to see peach and cherry blossoms, wisteria and peony blooms.

Chinese wisteria (Wisteria sinensis) covers the bridge in Liu Yuan, The Lingering Garden.

1. Yu Yuan, Garden of Contentment or Jade Garden

Located in the heart of old Shanghai, this jewel from the 16th century is surrounded by, yet secluded from, China's exploding 21st century. Who could fail to be attracted by this collection of everything Chinoise: cloud rocks, water, trees, flowers, pavilions, dragons, vases, walls, lattice windows and moon gates! Yu Yuan has it all, and in a condensed space. In 1982 the garden was named a National Place of Historic and Cultural Significance.

Timeline: 1560

Description

We visited Yu Yuan on the May Day holiday when it was full of thousands of tourists from rural China. We celebrated this special holiday together by wandering through the garden, feeding the fish and admiring the views.

Yu Yuan has been a resilient survivor of a turbulent 450-year history. Built in 1560 by the Pan Family, it thrived until 1760 when the family's fortunes waned. It was reborn as a merchant centre and then deteriorated again in 1880. It was destroyed when the Japanese invaded Shanghai in 1942. Good fortune saw its restoration in 1956.

We love its iconic design elements, especially the much-copied dragon-topped wall and the carved stone bridges and walkways. (A copy of the dragon wall was donated to the Garden of Friendship in Sydney's Darling Harbour on the occasion of the Australian Bicentenary in 1988.) And we love the exquisite detail in the pavilions; these architectural masterpieces appear to float on clouds of giant rock.

Don't miss …

» … the Zigzag Bridge with its teahouse in the middle, which many people believe inspired the Willow Pattern design (nice story but not true).

» … the wood-carved fruits and vegetables inside the entry hall.

» …the 12-metre mountains of stone, the work of Ming Dynasty Master Stonemason, Zhang Nanyang (hard to miss).

» … the 400-year-old ginkgo tree.

Best time to visit

This is not a primarily flower garden but April is a must see for the wisteria, peach, cherry blossom, jasmine and peonies. In October and November you'll catch the foliage trees in colour and in January and February the camellias are in flower.

Garden details

32 Anren Street, Shanghai
Open 1 Apr–June, 1 Sept–Nov; 8.30am–5pm
Tel +86 21 6328 2465
Size 2 hectares

Left: Enter through a bridge to the teahouse, the zigzag design is said to keep away the evil spirits.
Above: Traditional Chinese cloud topiary of Buxus planted in front of the dragon wall.

2. Zhuo Zheng Yuan, The Garden of the Humble Administrator

Four hours by train from Shanghai is Suzhou, a city known as the 'Venice of the East' due to the network of canals that crisscross the city. This garden, Suzhou's largest, has evolved with a special charm of its own through six centuries of construction and destruction. It has been awarded more heritage honours than any other Chinese classical garden and is UNESCO World Heritage listed.

Timeline: 1509

Description:

Picturesque covered walkways, corridors and stone bridges are built around a beautiful lake. The 16th-century fruit and vegetable gardens tended by the Humble Administrator have gone but informal gardens of flowers and shrubs have taken their place and groves of bamboo fill in the corners. In summer, weeping willows and camphor laurels offer welcome shade, and waterlilies and lotus cover interconnecting ponds filled with lazy giant koi carp. Timber corridors and pavilions are built over the ponds and larger lakes. In spring, the scene is awash with azalea, peony and hippeastrum.

We love the courtyard of camellias in the Eighteen Camellia Hall; you will find it in the western sector. The Ming and Qing Dynasty-era halls and pavilions that were once the homes of the owners are a real treat. This is Suzhou's largest garden and you need to allow at least two hours to stroll through, and yes it's always popular.

Don't miss …

» … the main roofed walkway, which affords a perspective of the garden's snake-like plan.

» … the Little Flying Rainbow, which is Suzhou's only covered garden bridge.

» … every latticework window because each one takes a special view.

… the pebble pathways, which are inlaid with Chinese symbols such as bats, cranes and coins.

» … the collection of 500 penjing and bonsai plants in the western area of the garden.

Best time to visit

April: The Azalea Festival coincides with new spring foliage of willows and maples and the wisteria is in bloom

August: Lotus time and the bonsai/penjing display

September: Chrysanthemum displays

January–February: Exhibition of orchids

Garden details

178 Dongbei Street, Suzhou

Open 1 Mar–31 May; 1 Sept–30 Nov; 1 Jun–31 Aug; 1 Dec–30 Apr;
8.15am–4.15pm

Tel +86 512 6751 0286

Size 5 hectares

Nearby you can visit Shizilin Yuan (Lion's Grove Garden)

Left: Spring brings the new red foliage of maples and brilliant displays of azaleas.
Right: Wisteria and azaleas flower in unison during April.
Next page left: Latticework windows frame beautiful views within the 700m long winding corridor.
Next page right: The new foliage of willow and camphor laurel brings welcome shade.

3. Liu Yuan, The Lingering Garden

This is China's finest garden, located in the centre of Suzhou and surrounded by whitewashed, plane tree-lined canals. It incorporates traditional architecture and landscape design and features mature trees, shrubs, climbers and perennials. UNESCO listed Liu Yuan in 1997 as one of the finest classical Ming Chinese gardens. You will want to linger here as long as possible.

Timeline: 1593, rebuilt 1930

Description

This is our favourite garden in China with beautifully grown wisterias, shrubs and trees. A narrow, whitewashed passage, 50 metres long, twists and turns past tiny open spaces. A long, covered, timber corridor, 700 metres in length, offers views from each individually designed window. We love the views of the main pool with its bridge dripping with two varieties of mauve wisteria blooms. In spring, the lime foliage of willow and bamboo and the inky darkness of the water provides the perfect foil for the mauve wisteria.

The gardens are divided roughly into four sections and feature 43 buildings in all. Our favourite is the Hall of Eminent Elders, which is ingeniously designed and built and offers China's best example of two completely different houses built under one roof.

Linger in the waterside pavilions to drink in the serenity and views of this magnificent garden. Capture great views of ducks, golden carp and overhanging foliage. Enjoy the collection of unusually shaped rocks.

Don't miss …

» … three giant 300-year-old ginkgo trees.

» … Cloud-Crowned Peak, a stunning 6.5-metre Taihu rock weighing five tonnes, which was intended for the Emperor's Imperial Garden.

» … glimpses of Suzhou's famous Tiger Hill Pagoda in the borrowed landscape beyond.

Left: Wisteria-covered zigzag bridge with carved timber balustrade.
Above: Help is on hand to keep the water clean.
Next page left: Harmony is achieved with the balance of rocks, pavilions, water and foliage.
Next page right: Wisteria sinensis.

Best time to visit

April: Maples, willows and ginkgos bursting into new growth and wisterias in bloom
June–July: Hydrangeas and oleanders in full flower
September: Chrysanthemums in flower and on display

Garden details

338 Liuyuan Road, Changmen Gate, Suzhou, Jiangsu
Open 1 Mar–31 May; 1 Sept–30 Nov; 1 Jun–31 Aug; 1 Dec–30 Apr; 7.30am–5pm
Tel +86 512 6557 9466
Size 2.3 hectares

4. Wang Shi Yuan, Master of the Fishing Nets Garden

The design of this Song-dynasty Suzhou house and garden, with its central lake, is a stunning example of perfectly proportioned open and closed spaces. Begun in 1140AD, the garden has had many owners and many re-designs in its long history. Visit early in the morning to escape the crowds so that you can fully appreciate the architecture, plants and the high standard of maintenance.

Timeline: 1140, rebuilt 1953

Description

This garden is smaller than most and too many visitors can make it feel crowded. So arrive early, be patient and you'll come away with stunning photographs.

Originally this garden was called Fisherman's Retreat, so you'll guess there is a large lake. It's surrounded by covered pathways, corridors, latticework windows, rocks, beautiful trees and pavilions. Indeed, this is possibly the most photographed pavilion of any in China's gardens, loved for its gentle proportions and modest spirit. The entire garden is well proportioned with 22 traditional buildings perfectly positioned with 'air' or space between them. This, along with cleverly placed mirrors on distant walls and masterly design, creates the illusion of a larger space. The many latticed windows offer views within views and scenes within scenes, borrowing the landscape from beyond.

Don't miss …

» … the Peony Cottage courtyard that was copied for the Ming Hall in the New York Metropolitan Museum of Art. The soapstone carvings above the doorways are particularly impressive.

» … the Moon Comes with the Breeze Pavilion with swooping eaves and trellised seats, which is a must for a moment of quiet reflection.

» … the smell of the Osmanthus Pavilion in autumn.

Best time to visit

April: Flowering wisteria and bamboo

June–July: Camellias in flower

Garden details

11 Kuojiatao Alley, Suzhou, Jiangsu

Open daily, 8am–5pm

Tel +86 512 6529 6567

Size 0.47 hectares

Left: Flowers and foliage soften outcrops of yellow huangshi granite.
Right: The Moon Comes with Breeze Pavilion is a charming place to sit.

5. Guozhuang, Guo's Villa

Escape the crowds of West Lake and immerse yourself in one of the best-kept secrets Hangzhou has to offer. Nothing can prepare you for what lies beyond the high walls of Guozhuang. We think this is the best example of a traditional private garden in China.

Timeline: 1851, rebuilt 1991

'In heaven there is Paradise,
On earth there is Suzhou and Hangzhou.'   Chinese Proverb

Description

Situated on the shores of West Lake, this garden was built by Guo Zhang in 1851, it's known as Guo's or Fenyang Villa and was heavenly restored and opened to the public in 1991, now it has grown into perfection.

Our groups repeatedly say Guo's Villa is their favorite in all China. Maybe it's the traditional buildings of a domestic scale that are set around the vast expanses of water filled with summer waterlilies or lotus flowers or the Japanese maples that absolutely radiate colour in the new spring leaf growth that captures the imagination. Being placed adjacent to a magical acreage of stunningly landscaped parkland alongside West Lake filled with a vast forest of once rare Metasequoia trees also can't but help.

The immediate views across from the shoreline of West Lake are possibly the key to unlocking Guo's Villa magic. The villa faces Spring Dawn at the Su Causeway, which spans West Lake. With Twin Peaks Piercing the Cloud in the west, it commands a distant view of the serene Southern Screen Hill and the graceful Baochu Pagoda. Don't rush your visit and definitely take the exit into the shady park next door, which is filled with massed shrub plantings and the largest group of 30-year-old metasequoia trees in China.

Don't miss …

» … the camphor laurel, holly and celtis trees, which are original and more than 700 years old.

» … enjoy Chinese tea and a packed lunch on one of the garden's lakeside pavilions, look out over the entire West lake, past Su Causeway and on to downtown Hangzhou. The view is incredible, the breeze is fresh and the location is quiet.

» … 'Living in Quietness', which is where the host used to live and meet guests. The rooms are tastefully furnished with antique furniture.

» … 'The Sky in the Mirror' garden section with corridors, stone bridges and rockeries as well as trees and flowers surround the sky-mirrored pond in the centre.

» … board the dragon boat, near Heartbroken Bridge for a ride on West Lake. Through a misty sky, admire the bridges edged with graceful weeping willow trees and the lake is bordered with yellow water iris and filled with lotus.

Best time to visit

April: Fresh lime growth of weeping willows, pink peach flowers at the waters edge and surprising beds of tulips
June–July: Lotus in full flower in the lakes and ponds

Garden details

Nan Shan Lu, Hangzhou, Zhejiang
Open daily

Left: Whitewashed walls enhance leafy reflections.
Above right: Exit through a planting of Metasequoia.
Below right: Open pavilion with upswept roof provides a charming outlook.

Japan

Japanese gardens are different to those of other Asian cultures. Gardens are aged between 500 and 700 years, younger than those of continental Asia and far more complex in design. These contemplative gardens were inspired by Zen Buddhist philosophy, the patronage of the shoguns and their samurai and the wealth of successful merchants.

Garden gazing in Japan is a serious business with several thousand choices: 'One for every day of your life'. To maximise your experience, be mindful of the need for reflection and contemplation. Leave your worries at the door! Japanese gardens possess a unique serenity based on impeccable design, brilliant plant selection and excellent maintenance.

We first went to Japan in 1980 and have been taking tours every year since. We have found the Japanese standard of horticulture to be unsurpassed and inspirational, setting the gardens apart from those elsewhere. We visit early April for cherry blossoms and mid-November for fall's fiery foliage.

Cherry blossom time at Mt Fuji.

6. Kenrokuen

This is our favourite strolling garden. Its history, complex design, horticulture and sheer beauty make it number one. Water is a major element of this large garden, built between 1670 and 1870 for the Maeda Clan warlord friends of the Tokagawa Shogun. The garden's beautiful trees, classic stone lanterns and bridges are Japan's finest.

Timeline: 1670

Description

The Chinese name means 'Combining Six Attributes': spaciousness, seclusion, design, antiquity, water and vistas. Perched on Kodatsuno Plateau in Kanazawa City, the 11.4-hectare garden is dominated by the 5000 square metre Misty Pond. Japan's tallest man-made waterfall spills 6.6 metres into the smaller Gourd Pond (1774). Of the 18 stone lanterns, the uneven two-legged Kotoji lantern, standing behind a bowed 5-metre stone bridge, is the symbol of Kenroku-en and Kanazawa.

In drier months, the meandering streams are kept looking 'wet' with massed blue iris, a scene described as 'perfect' by the masters. The most magnificent of the dozen bridges, Flying Wild Geese Longevity Bridge, has 11, six-sided stone slabs creating its steps. In winter, many of the 11,800 mature pines have their branches supported by Yukitsuri maypoles with rope for protection against heavy snowfalls. Spring flowering cherries are exceptionally beautiful in this garden. One cherry is 750 years old!

Our favourite tree, the famous Karasaki Pine, which is supported by submerged bamboo stakes, across Misty Pond and has grown 8 metres in 30 years.

Don't miss …

» … the beautifully restored Seisonkaku Villa which was built in 1863 by a lord for his mother and features a timber structure with no nails, 'nightingale' floors, rare painted upstairs rooms and exquisite displays.

» … Japan's first fountain (1859), which rises four metres by water pressure from the river 10 kilometres away.

Best time to visit

March: Plum blossoms

April: 400 cherry trees flower

May: Flowering iris and azaleas

October–November: Autumn maples and zelkova trees colour

November–December: Pine trees have winter rope supports against snow damage

Garden details

1 Kenroku-machi, Kanazawa, Ishikawa

Open 1 Mar–15 Oct, 7am–6pm; 16 Oct–28 Feb, 8am–4.30pm

Tel +81 076 234 3800

Size 11.4 hectares

Left: Bamboo frames support pine tree branches from the heavy weight of snow.
Above right: Uneven two-legged kotoji lattern is the symbol of the garden and the symbol of the city.
Below right: Cherry blossom time in April.

7. Ryoan-ji

Never has so much been written about 15 rocks. Your interpretation of the placement of Ryoan-ji's famous rocks will depend on the teachings of Buddha, Zen philosophy—or your imagination. Every Westerner we've introduced to the Rock Garden of Ryoan-ji agrees this garden is magical and mysterious. Myriad copies of the garden exist around the globe but the original must be seen.

Timeline: 1430–73, restored 1488, gravel garden 1525

'I only learn to be content .'

Description

Everyone tries to interpret the meaning of the white raked quartz and the 15 stones but we believe there isn't one. When we stood atop Yashima Plateau on Shikoku Island in 1980 we immediately thought, yes, the islands of the Inland Sea of Japan, the inspiration for the stones at Ryoan-ji. It is, but then again, it isn't; the garden is whatever you think it is, that's Zen. This garden is the most famous Zen Buddhist creation on earth. Empty your mind and meditate on these rocks.

There is much that tourists overlook here. The 256 square metre Dry Garden, built in 1525, is miniscule in size to the surrounding 48-ha Wet Garden outside with its massive 12th century Mirror Pond. The cherry blossom trees, the maples, the conifers, the enormous wisteria arbour and the serenity and flow of the entire garden makes this place a joy to visit. Don't be rushed by your guide. Follow the map to the full extent of the outer garden.

Don't miss …

» … the Rock Garden walls, made from mud and boiled oil, have become an amazing artwork but look at the perspective; it's an intentional illusion.

» … the carved stone washbasin or Tsukubai behind the main temple offers this advice: 'I only learn to be content'.

» … a rare stand of Kyoto's very own variety of *Cryptomeria japonica* beyond the lake.

Best time to visit

April: The spring cherry blossom
May: The wisteria arbour in full flower
November: The maples in full autumn colour

Garden details

13 Goryonoshita-cho, Ryoan-ji, Ukyo-ku, Kyoto
Open 1 Mar–30 Nov, 8am–5pm; Dec–28 Feb, 8.30am–4.30pm
Tel +81 075 463 2216
Size 48 hectares

Left: Objects of meditation.
Above: Restaurant view in autumn.

8. Saiho-ji, The Moss Temple

You must apply in writing to visit Kyoto's famous Moss Garden many months in advance. Those lucky enough to gain entry walk on paths through lush moss, which is lit with a shimmering tracery of light falling through the trees overhead. In the autumn, the garden is ablaze with maples, their reflections burning in the lake. It is one of the oldest surviving gardens in Japan, founded in the eighth century; its present layout dates from the 14th century.

Timeline: 729, 1167, present garden 1338

Description

It took us years to gain access to this garden in the 1980s but it was worth the wait. Be prepared, you too may not gain entry first time to this 1.8-hectare masterpiece. Time and nature have overlaid the original design to make a place of tranquility in this, one of Japan's oldest gardens. There are more than 120 types of moss flourishing beneath a canopy of mature conifers and maples. The ponds and streams complete the picture. The garden was UNESCO World Heritage listed in 1994. The garden was commenced in 729 but the major design was by Saint Enro who added the huge pond in 1167. It was changed in 1338 by revered Zen priest, Muso Kokushi, only to be damaged by fire, flood and neglect throughout the 18th century. Nature then played her hand, introducing mosses, which were encouraged by Kyoto's oppressively wet and humid subtropical summers. The result of this 1200-year-old team effort is mesmerising.

Before you can enter you must take part in a meditative Buddhist ceremony. This preparation stills the spirit and enhances your experience of the garden. The garden is small in size but huge in impact so walk slowly and try to absorb every aspect, pond ripple, vista and moss leaf.

Don't miss …

» … Muso's original rock garden, the world's first garden rockery.
» … the Shonantei tea ceremony house, which dates from the 16th century and is an official Japanese Cultural Relic.
» … the rare flowering cyclamen.

Best time to visit

April–May–June: Garden looks its best with cool but sunny days
October–November: Maples in colour

Garden details

56 Jingatani-cho, Nishikyo-ku, Matsuo, Kamigatani-cho, Kyoto
Open apply in writing
Tel +81 075 391 3631
Size 1.8 hectares

Left: Carpets of verdant moss ripple with age.
Above: Moss-covered bridge gives a timeless quality.

9. Korakuen

This is one of Japan's most celebrated gardens, a spacious, grand landscape that was magnificently restored after World War II, along with the nearby city of Okayama. Korakuen contains all the elements of a fine Japanese garden: streams, waterfalls, bridges, shrines, teahouses, rocks, flowers, trees, open sky, expansive lawns and a magnificent castle.

Timeline: 1687

Description

Commenced by daimyo Lord Ikeda in 1687, Korakuen took 13 years to build but was completely destroyed in World War II. Master gardeners, with access to original drawings, accurately reconstructed the buildings and the gardens. Since 1980, we've experienced many magical moments here: traditional kimono-clad ladies with colourful umbrellas; white swans with a family of cygnets sailing on the pond; eating fresh strawberries while relaxing on the lawns listening to live koto music; sighting rare Japanese cranes; joining locals in a tea ceremony in the quaint tea house; and a wedding.

As you stroll through this 'master' garden you will encounter delightful horticultural treats: the curtain of wisteria in front of the shop, the 6m hill of azaleas, the stream lined with beautiful Japanese iris, ladies harvesting tea in the miniature plantation. And with the dramatic Black Crow Castle of Okayama in the background—it's a photographer's dream.

Don't miss …

» … the 100-tree maple forest, the weeping flowering cherry tree in the rear garden near the timber bridge, the Cycad Garden and the Noh theatre stage.

» … the rear of the house and the unique Zig Zag bridge with iris flowering below.

Best time to visit

April: 100 perfumed Plum Grove trees flowering
April–May: Catch the weeping cherry blossoms
May–June: Iris flowers
June–August: Ancient Oga lotus bloom
Late November: Autumn colour

Garden details

1–5 Koraku-en, Okayama-shi, Okayama
Open every day from Apr–Sept, 7.30am–6pm;
Oct–Mar, 8am–5pm
Tel +81 (086) 272 1148
Size 13.3 hectares

Left: A zigzagged wooden bridge leads through Korakuen.
Above: Japanese water iris accentuate the colour of the stream.

10. Ginkaku-ji, Temple of the Silver Pavilion

Kinkaku-ji, the Golden Pavilion, is covered with gold leaf, so you might expect the Silver Pavilion, Ginkaku-ji, to be silver. It's not but it is a beautiful garden. It has great landscape features: sculptured trees, flowing streams, weathered rocks, velvet moss, rare camellias and the manicured hill behind makes this a must visit. The huge mound and 'pond' of shimmering white sand are great too.

Timeline: 1482

Description

Shogun Yoshimasa built a home on this site for his retirement in 1482, but he died before it could be covered in silver. After his death, the villa became a Buddhist temple. The famous Sand Garden, a huge, conical mound of sand (said to symbolise Mount Fuji) with shimmering raked white quartz was a later addition by a samurai. The sand reflects the moonlight and illuminates the garden at night. Maybe this is another reason why it's called the 'Silver' Pavilion.

The lower gardens are well preserved with exquisite views across the pond to the Togudo (Hall of Eastern Quest) giving a lyrical beauty that is in stark contrast to the 'Silver Sand Sea'. The various buildings within this historic garden saw the beginnings of modern Japanese culture: the tea ceremony, Zen philosophy and the study of art, ceramics, Noh theatre and architecture.

Once past the striking white gravel at the entrance, the garden unfolds with narrow pathways taking you on a great experience past iconic stone bridges. Note the camellias, exquisitely pruned Japanese pine trees, ginkgos and old maples. Be sure to visit the new Visitors Centre and note the intricate detail of the timber structure. The hill path is new and difficult but the view of Kyoto and the Temple and garden is worth every step.

Don't miss …

» … the unique 50-metre entrance walk of camellia hedge, rock and bamboo walling, which is a journey to clear the mind for the paradise beyond.

» … the opportunity to look up on the hill to see thousands of manicured mature *Cryptomeria* cedars.

» … the Philosopher's Walk nearby, full of flowering cherries in April.

Best time to visit

April–June: Azaleas

July–September: Temperature is hot but the garden is still stunning

October–late November: Autumn maple and ginkgo foliage

December–February: A snowy wonderland

Garden details

2 Ginkakuji-cho, Sakyou-ku, Kyoto

Open daily 8.40am–5pm (to 4.30pm in winter)

Tel +81 075 771 5725

Left: An impressive entrance where quartz reflects the moonlight and illuminates the garden at night.
Above: The first pond coloured with maples for autumn.

11. Hakusasonso

This is not a grand garden but a beautifully proportioned, peaceful stroll garden created by Japanese artist Hashimoto Kansetsu in 1916. Beyond its borders, thousands of visitors head to Ginkaku-ji Temple. The garden features a large collection of ancient Chinese stone lanterns, pagodas and Buddhas and an eclectic range of trees and shrubs surround the reflection pond, all set against the backdrop of Mt Daimonji.

Timeline: 1916

Description

It's a rare treat to visit a large private garden in Kyoto. There are very few private gardens open to the public as land is highly valuable and sought after. A visit here is a real eye-opener.. It was once the home of the famous Japanese artist Hashimoto Kansetsu, who spent his life painting, designing his gardens and teahouses and collecting stone pagodas. His art hangs in galleries in Tokyo, Paris and Boston. Kansetsu visited China more than 40 times and developed a love of Chinese art, landscape, culture and aesthetics. This is reflected in his paintings and in the garden design. He collected important Persian and Greek art, which is on display in the garden museum.

Today Hashimoto Kansetsu's family cares for the garden and the traditional buildings. Mrs Hashimoto, a Master of the Tea Ceremony, conducts the multi-faceted traditional ceremony that is strongly influenced by Zen Buddhism. This ethereal experience should not be missed. A meandering stream flows through the garden opening into a large reflection pond, a sheet of water between the tea house and a small pavilion. If time permits, enjoy exquisite cuisine in the restaurant—it will be a meal to remember.

Don't miss …

» … Hashimoto's Stone, which is engraved, 'My spirit of art, must be free'.

» … the Kunisaki Stone Tower, which is Japan's tallest.

» … the rare Chinese *Pinus bungeana* and old crepe myrtle trees.

» … the bamboo grove with an unusual collection of stone Buddhas.

Best time to visit

April–May: Spring blossom

October–December: Autumn colours

February–March: Winter blooms include camellias and magnolias

Garden details

30 Jodoji, Ishibashi-cho, Sakyo-ku, Kyoto City

Open all year round

Tel +81 075 751 0446

office@kansetu.or.jp

Left: Stone steps lead across the pond to the teahouse.
Above: The tallest Chinese pagoda in Japan.

Indonesia

North of Broome the tropical waters of the Indian Ocean take us to the tiny island of Bali. The warm waves gently lap at the shore as fishermen make their offerings each day, asking blessings from the gods and goddesses. The tropical sea is alive with marine life flitting between mushroom coral, twisted brain coral and triffid-like seaweed.

Here is a country whose friendly people are mindful of each sacred moment; a country where daily ritual, religious beliefs and family are unified. The ancient culture is rooted in reverence, respect, balance and karma. Hidden here are some of the world's most beautiful tropical gardens. The tropical Bali style of garden design is much copied around the world.

Bali has a true tropical climate with a distinct wet and dry season. The landscapes of Bali have become synonymous with tropical holidays and the Balinese style of garden design. Frangipanis and other tropical flowers and trees such as gingers, heliconias, ixora and lotus have become much coveted throughout the world.

Sacred lotus (Nelumbo nucifera) light up the water's surface.

12. Tirtagangga, Water Palace

'Tirta' means holy water and 'Gangga' means the Ganges river, locals believing the water in the garden flows from the holy Indian river. Tirtagangga is a small village in the eastern part of the island of Bali, two hours from Bali International airport and 15 kilometres north of Amlapura. This is one of three water palaces in east Bali, built as a holy spring. Much of the water palace was destroyed by the 1963 volcanic eruption but what has survived is mesmerising and it's worth tearing yourself away from your resort for an unforgettable day trip.

Timeline: 1947

Description

'Tirtha' is a pilgrimage site signifying a shallow body of water that may be easily crossed, the journey symbolising the crossing from worldly pleasures to Nirvana. This garden is worth your own personal pilgrimage to a water wonderland made up of several water ponds that can be crossed by inviting pathways of hand-carved stepping-stones, dotted with enthusiastic water fountains and surrounded by rambunctious tropical gardens full of colourful bougainvillea and desert rose (*Adenium*). A holy water swimming pool fed by natural springs is a must for a refreshing dip.

Tirtagangga was created by Anak Agung Anglurah, the former Raja or last King of Karangasem, who also built a much larger water palace in the north-east of Bali, Ujung, which was destroyed by earthquake in 1979 and subsequently rebuilt. In comparison Tirtagangga is a smaller pocket-sized palace and is a surprising sanctuary—a world away from the hustle of the surrounding streets.

Those staying in *Candi Dasa* or *Tenganan*, will find an afternoon swim in Tirtagangga a perfect cool off; the round trip taking 45 minutes. For those hiking up to Bali's scenic temple, *Pura Lempuyang*, a swim at Tirtagangga is the perfect finish to your trek.

Don't miss …

» … the large traveller's palms (*Ravenala madagascariensis*).

» … the Genta Bali restaurant next door has a guide who can escort you around the garden and provide information unavailable to the average tourist.

» … a stay within the water palace at the Marble Villa or Lion Villa. Both are shaded by a 500-year-old Banyan Tree.

» … Ryoshi teahouse perched up on the cliff for refreshments and a great view.

Best time to visit

Dry season (June–August) is best and we recommend timing your visit for the morning to get the most out of a swim in the holy water pools.

Garden details

Not far from Denpasar, take a bus from Batubulan to Amlapura then a bemo to Tirtagangga.

Tirtagangga Water Palace, Amlapura, Karangasem 80811, Bali, Indonesia
Open daily 7am–6pm
Tel +62 363 21 383

Left: Interactive, a garden for all ages.
Above: The holy waters of the spring have been channelled into stone basins.

13. The Bali Hyatt

This was one of Made Wijaya's first gardens and started a Balinese school of garden design that has spread through the tropical world. Distinctive architecture is surrounded by lush tropical gardens with exotic foliage and secluded lily ponds.

Timeline: 1973, redesigned 1980

Description

For more than 50 years Sanur has been the favoured retreat for tourists and long-staying Bali lovers. Made famous by Australian artists, such as Donald Friend and Ian Fairweather during the 1960s and 1970s, Sanur's special village character was preserved by a government regulation that no building could be taller that the height of a mature coconut palm. The result is a superb collection of bungalow-style hotels and resorts, not to mention the most beautiful gardens.

In the middle of Sanur is the Bali Hyatt, one of Bali's landmark gardens, a world-famous creation. Originally built in 1973 on a former coconut grove, it was reworked in 1980 by landscape designer Made Wijaya. Bold expanses of mature coconut trees, flame trees and frangipanis contrast with more intimate areas. Sunny open gardens give way to soothing shade. Bold, tropical flowers are highlighted against restful foliages. This is a garden of contrast and balance. Red gingers, sweeps of purple-leafed rhoeo, ixora and sculptural stands of coconut palms flow in and out of well-designed pools and allow glimpses to the ocean beyond.

Don't miss …

» … a garden tour of the site.

» … the more intimate courtyard gardens.

» … the white garden, Made's tribute to Vita Sackville-West's Sissinghurst.

» … a dip in the spa!

Best time to visit

Any day of the year

Garden details

Jalan Danau Tamblingan 89, Sanur 80228

Open daily

Tel +62 361 28 1234

balihyatt.inquiries@hyattintl.com

Size 14.5 hectares

Left: Interior garden courtyard.
Above: Restaurant overlooks tropical gardens.

14. Pura Taman Kemuda Saraswati, The Lotus Temple

Enter off the busy street, through a traditional Balinese gate, cross a stone bridge over the lotus-filled pond to Pura Taman Kemuda Saraswati, the Lotus Temple. Located in the spiritual and geographic heart of Ubud, this peaceful retreat is filled with water, lotus and flanked with gigantic frangipani trees.

Timeline: 1950

Description

This garden has a magic that draws you in. Lotus flowers light the pond's surface, each flower an exquisite perfection. The lotus has long been seen as a powerful sacred symbol. Its emergence from the murky depths of a pool symbolises the rise of the soul out of darkness into the pure light of nirvana. Each bud swells and opens into a symmetrical circle of blush-pink petals, which open to unveil a golden core, reflecting the eternal cycle of life. Seed heads age to black to become sculptural remnants of love and beauty. The simultaneous appearance of seedpod, flower and bud conveniently suggests the past, present and future. Every part of the lotus from the underground tubers to the seeds is eaten.

The Puri Saraswati complex is devoted to Dewi Saraswati, the goddess of learning, literature and the arts. This is a stunning temple with commanding architecture but the real highlight is the water garden. The temple contains pools of blessed waters but be warned these waters often contain fish and other pond life (including eels). Watch for the resident owl.

We advise enlisting the help of a Balinese friend or a friendly hotel employee to take you to a temple ceremony and advise you about what is taking place and how you can appreciate and participate in the ceremony without making a faux pas.

Don't miss …

» … a meal at the Lotus Café, which overlooks the lotus ponds. The food is fresh and delicious. Dine the Asian way, on bamboo mats, overlooking lotus flowers in bloom. Twice a week (Tuesdays and Saturdays) you can watch performances of traditional Balinese dances and gamelan orchestras. At other times you may hear musicians in practice or witness one of Ubud's frequent temple ceremonies in progress.

» … the fine padmasana (lotus throne).

Best time to visit

Any day of the year—the lotus flower continually in this climate.

Garden details

Jalan Raya, Ubud

Open daily except during ceremonies

Before you attend any religious ceremony or enter a temple, observe the strict etiquette and dress code.

Left: Edible fruit pod develops in the centre.
Above: The stone bridge with water fountains leads to the temple.

Thailand

Thailand, with its sultry climate and monsoonal weather patterns, is home to a wide variety of plants. Those passionate about palms, frangipani, cordyline and heliconia will have Thailand high on their list of must-see destinations. Thailand is heaven for tropical plant lovers who come from all over the world to relish warm weather and world-class tropical resorts.

Thai gardens have a unique style of grace and serenity. Tropical plant lovers will dine on a feast of fecundity, festoon of flowers and charming ornamentation. Gardens in the south are lush, tropical retreats with jungle plantings that seem to grow in front of your eyes. Nong Nooch Tropical Botanic Garden is the best example of its type in the world, far outclassing other tropical botanic gardens with its sheer size—a botanical Disneyworld with rides! .

Intensive breeding of frangipani has resulted in thousands of new cultivars.

15. Nong Nooch Tropical Botanic Garden

This is the Kew Gardens of Thailand that borrows horticultural styles from all over the world. It's an East meets West extravaganza, a living circus, in the southern province of Chonburi on the Gulf of Thailand. It's tropical Disneyland with elephant rides!

Timeline: 1980

Description

When you arrive at the gardens you notice the endless scenes of various palms and tropical plants, giant greenhouses and shade structures, impeccably sculpted shrubs and trees, brilliant colours in every direction and an amazing tidiness that is astounding for such a huge garden.

Our fascination with Nong Nooch Botanic Gardens lies in its world-class collection of tropical plants including cycads, palms, climbers and one of Asia's largest private collections of frangipanis. It's a plant lover's paradise! Extensive collections of other tropical plants such as cordylines, crotons, bougainvillea, passionfruit, canna, heliconia and gingers will delight tropical plant lovers. The garden includes an extensive collection of 500 frangipani varieties, many have been bred within Thailand and exist nowhere else.

In 1954, Mr Pisit and Mrs Nongnooch Tansacha purchased the land for the conservation of tropical plants and the growing of mangoes, oranges, coconuts and other local fruits. However after a tour of the gardens of the world Mrs Nongnooch was inspired to turn her fruit orchard into a tropical botanic garden full of ornamental flowers and plants. The garden was later turned into a tourist attraction with all the trimmings.

Don't miss …

» … a formal water cascade of epic proportions.
» … the French parterre garden an exquisitely-manicured area with perfect borders and a riot of colour.
» … an adaptation of Stonehenge.
» … the only garden we know in which you can see by elephant!
» … more than 500 species of palms from Asia, Madagasca, New Caledonia and America including a few that are nearly extinct in the wild.

Best time to visit

Any time

Garden details

34/1 Sukhumvit Hgw, Najomtien, Sattahip 20250
Pattaya, Chonburi
Open daily 8am–6pm
Tel +66 38 70 9358-62
www.nongnoochtropicalgarden.com
Size 500 acres

Left: Sculptured hedges in this topiary garden are kept in shape with regular pruning.
Above: The French parterre garden.

Chapter 2

GREAT BRITAIN

Great Britain is Mecca for garden lovers. We come from all over the world to savour horticulture at its best. The Royal Horticulture Society ensures the education and aspiration of generations of gardeners, plant breeders, horticulturists, garden owners and visitors. The National Trust is the custodian of this unrivalled living heritage. Great Britain has more gardens, both private and public, than any other part of the world. You could visit a different garden every day of the year. The National Trust cares for more than 300 houses and gardens all opened for everyone to enjoy. Join up for discounted entry. The English cottage style with roses, herbaceous borders and walls smothered with flowering climbers is truly inspirational. You will see great gardens of all sizes, from flowering pub ball baskets to grand parkland landscapes.

Sissinghurst, the most popular garden in England, is famous for its many garden rooms.

England

Every gardener in England has the chance to rest in winter, curl up with a stockpile of garden books and plan the season ahead. English gardens are well planned, even meticulous! So it is no wonder the whole world copies the English garden style. It's a flower-fest with garden borders filled with colour, blossom and fragrance. The horticulture is exemplary, the cultivation so intense that floral displays change through each week of each season. This means you can visit these gardens from spring to autumn and always see something special.

Britain has more gardens, both private and public, than any other country. You could travel around Britain visiting glorious gardens every day of the year. The National Trust cares for 215 houses and gardens, all open for everyone to enjoy. Join up for discounted entry. The English cottage style with roses, herbaceous borders and walls smothered with flowering climbers is inspirational. You will see great gardens of all sizes, from flowering pub ball baskets to grand parkland landscapes.

The tradition in garden making continues into the 21st century with innovative young designers at the annual Chelsea Flower Show in London showcasing their talents to a worldwide audience. Don't miss it! We recommend joining up to the Royal Horticultural Society to allow you entry on Members Day—this is the only way to see Chelsea!

The long border leading up to the house at Great Dixter.

16. Beth Chatto Garden

One and three quarters of an hour drive from London is the private garden of garden designer and writer, Beth Chatto. This well known plantswoman has planted her garden by selecting 'the right plant for the right place' and it's for this reason her garden shines. Plants in her garden are so carefully nurtured that they grow as close to perfection as is possible.

Timeline: 1960

'If you choose plants adapted by nature to the conditions you have to offer, they will do well, and the garden will give you a sense of peace and fulfilment.'

Beth Chatto

Description

On a parcel of dry east-country land, unfit even for farming, are the famous gardens of Beth Chatto. Best known is the Gravel Garden, once a car park, now Beth's highly successful and much-copied experiment in dry climate gardening. Planted as a sequence of island beds that expand and shrink with the luxuriant growth of perennials, it reaches a peak in summer. A tapestry of colours is woven using drought-tolerant Mediterranean plants that are never watered. We love the plant friendships: the electric blue sea holly (Eryngium) planted with lime euphorbia and orange alstroemeria; English lavender with yellow yarrow; a timber bench swamped in pink lavatera and thistle; and fragile red Flanders poppies floating beside spiky agaves.

There is a dramatic change as you step down into a lush leafy water garden, in all shades of green. This garden of moisture-loving plants is designed around a chain of ponds fed by a cool natural spring. Pond margins are home to iris, flowering rush and astilbes.

The woodland garden shows how the dry area beneath large mature English oaks can be transformed with winter snowdrops, spring daffodils, hellebores and violets, summer grasses and autumn crocus and cyclamen.

The woodland is at its peak in spring but can also be appreciated in autumn when the trees are in a blaze of glory and the shrubs show off their colourful berries.

There's a lesson here for every gardener; find the plant that best suits the location. It's one of the leading principles of ecological gardening.

Don't miss …

» … crossing the ponds to the far side of the garden, where grow a million shades and tones of green. Sit there and commit the scene to memory.

» … the 'Scree' garden, a series of raised beds with smaller plants that would be lost in the main garden.

» … the Gravel Garden for those who wish to garden with nature, not struggle against her.

Best time to visit

» There are many glorious flowering plants in this garden, especially in spring, with dogwood, magnolia, cercis and viburnum all in flower. Opinions are divided about the best time because summer is the peak time for perennials in the Gravel Garden. But it's the greens of the Water Garden that really inspire us all year round – Green Tapestry, the title Beth Chatto gave to her first book.

Garden details

Elmstead Market, Colchester, Essex CO 7 7DB
6km east of Colchester
Open Mar–Oct, Mon–Sat, 9am–5pm; Nov–Feb, Mon–Fri, 9am–4pm
Closed Sundays
Tel +44 (0)1206 822007
www.bethchatto.co.uk

Left: The dry gravel garden is never watered.
Above: A chain of ponds make up the water garden.

17. Hidcote Manor

Just an hour out of Oxford at the top of the rolling Cotswolds is one of England's finest gardens, Hidcote Manor, now held in the safe hands of the National Trust. Its 'Arts and Crafts' style has influenced generations of gardeners. It's a clever and interesting garden of 12 'rooms', each with its own character. American-born British soldier and garden creator, Major Lawrence Johnston, moved to Hidcote in 1907 and pioneered this style in the United Kingdom.

Timeline: 1907

Description

We love the way this complex series of garden spaces is revealed as you explore. Each space is enclosed; some spaces are crowded and intense, other spaces are open and expansive. At no one point can you see it all. Intersecting axes provide enchanting vistas and the visitor is given enticing glimpses into adjoining 'rooms', which open off corridors formed from 'walls' of yew and box, copper beech and hornbeam and are furnished with clipped statues of green topiary: birds; hens; peacocks; arches; and balls. Hedges on stilts make up the walls of the Stilt Garden.

The garden progresses through the seasons like the movements of a symphony. Layers of planting are revealed in sequence. The famous 'red' border is a good example. In early spring, red tulips are followed by red-flowered rhubarb, then red geum and poppies, followed by red roses, then cannas, salvias, daylilies and finally red dahlias. It's a grand performance that lasts for months. While you swoon, also admire the outstanding standard of the horticulture.

Don't miss ...

» ... behind the house for the greenhouse area, the kitchen garden and the old garden rose walk, decorated with clematis-covered columns and pillars of yew and backed with French lilacs, all leading to a fine pair of standard wisterias.

» ... the red borders, which date from 1913 and are said to be the first single-coloured borders in England. They glow with heart-stopping intensity in the soft light, especially when contrasted against deep green background hedges.

Left: Outdoor 'rooms' are linked by vistas and furnished with all sorts of topiary, most of them birds.
Above: The stilt garden with pleached hornbeams.
Next page left: Wisteria flank this iron bench in the Rose Borders, this part of the garden built 1907–1914.
Next page right: The original tree, Cedar of Lebanon is a giant guardian of the garden.

Best time to visit

This garden is impeccably maintained and looks great all year round, even in winter when a dusting of snow outlines the topiary.

Garden details

Hidcote Bartrim, Gloucestershire GL55 6LR
6.5km NW of Chipping Campden
Open Apr–Oct, Sat–Wed, 10.30am–6pm (5pm in Oct)
Tel +44 (0)1386 438333
www.nationaltrust.org.uk

18. Great Dixter

This is the garden of the late Christopher Lloyd (and originally his father. Nathaniel, who planted out the topiary). Christopher Lloyd challenged the 1930's mindset for pastel rose gardens by pulling out his roses, banishing pastels and injecting glorious colour. His gardening books are popular and have challenged gardeners to be brave with colour and to experiment with foliage and texture. There are hundreds of lessons here in his garden, from grand flower border designs to harmonious collections of potted plants. It's a tribute to the team at Dixter that this garden continues to shine!

Timeline: 1910

Description

The sheer drama of this garden is irresistible. There is a bold, unrestrained use of colour. Plants are allowed to self-seed to make happy garden pictures. The garden changes shape as the season progresses, becoming full and abundant with flower and foliage reaching a peak late in summer and then achieving a natural senescence in late autumn, with the intrinsic beauty of dried seed heads, grasses and spent fruits.

There are no segregated colour schemes here, instead a mix of what happens naturally is encouraged. Gardens are arranged in a circuit around the house. Of all the gardens within this complex, most enticing are the wide borders with their waves of flower and foliage. Best of the lot is the Long Border. No gaps appear along its length from May, when it comes into spring bloom, until the end of September. It's a study in flower shapes — umbels, spires, trumpets, asters and contrasting textural grasses. It looks exuberant and uncontrived, an image that belies the enormous horticultural skill required to achieve this effect. This is a gardener's garden!

Don't miss …

»   … the 'signature' yew topiary birds and peacocks that date to Christopher Lloyd's father's time and which seem to 'inhabit' rather than 'grow'. The birds, along with all the hedges, are pruned in August and retain their shape all year.

»   … the Sunken Garden which is surrounded by the Barn Garden with lovely views from all angles.

»   … the Brunswick fig espalier against one of the Barn walls, used for its foliage rather than its fruit.

Best time to visit

August: The whole garden has a summer exhuberance

Garden details

Dixter Rd, Northiam, Rye, East Sussex TN31 6PH

21km from Hastings

Open Apr–Oct, Tue–Sun, 2–5pm

Tel +44 (0)1797 252878

www.greatdixter.co.uk

Left: The sunken garden with clipped yew and flower borders during peak summer.
Above: Topiary peacocks in yew (Taxus) are remnants of the original garden.

19. Mottisfont Abbey

This 13th-century priory has a lovely walled garden (once the kitchen garden) that was chosen in 1972 by Graham Thomas, Britain's eminent rosarian, to house the National Collection of Old Roses for the National Trust. Graham Thomas was responsible for the revival of interest in 'Heritage' roses. Roses in this garden, climbers and shrub roses, were grown from his own collection of old, pre-1900 roses.

Timeline: 1972

Description

We have a particular love affair with old roses, Gallicas, Bourbons, tea roses, damasks, albas and hybrid perpetuals and this is a spectacular garden in which to enjoy them. Their season is short but stunning. Their fragrance, especially in the evening, is trapped in this walled garden, allowing the visitor to fully appreciate the breadth of scents. The roses have a heart-stopping exuberance, spilling over ponds, caught up in arbours, trained over arches and flattened against walls.

   There is a wonderful mix of roses and perennials, including softly coloured lavenders, pinks, lupins, foxgloves, geraniums and catmint. The honey-coloured stonewalls absorb the heat and contribute to the health and vigour of all the roses here, as well as providing a lovely backdrop.

Don't miss …

»   … a walk around the grounds, including the Abbey Stream. The 17th-century millstream takes you past the Great Plane Tree, thought to be the largest in the country. Close by, across the lawn is the spring (font) from which Mottisfont takes its name.

Best time to visit

A summer evening is best to fully appreciate the fragrance of the roses. The garden remains open into the evenings in June for this purpose.

Garden details

Mottisfont, Romsey, Hampshire
7km NW of Romsey
Open Mar–Oct, Sat–Wed, 11am–5pm, daily in Jun, 11am–8.30pm
Tel +44 (0)1794 340757
www.nationaltrust.org.uk

Left: 'Raubritter' rose spills over circular pond, while 'Adelaide d'Oleans' rambles over the arbour.
Above: Metal arch supports 'Adelaide d'Orleans' and the climbing rose over the wall is 'Bouquet d'Orleans'.

20. Nymans

Here is a great example of adversity changing a garden. Three generations of the Messel family owned Nymans from the 1890s to 1953 when it passed to the hands of the National Trust. Originally it was a collection of gardens with a pinetum, arboretum, rock garden, heather garden, Japanese garden and rhododendron garden; all have survived but not the house.

Timeline: 1890–1953

Description

The grand house at Nymans was destroyed by fire in 1947 so now it's a romantic ruin, smothered in wisteria, clematis and climbing roses. This picturesque scene, with a rose-covered dovecote alongside, sets the mood for the gardens around it.

A progression of flowers blooms through the seasons with magnolias and camellias in February, followed by woodland walks of bluebells in April, leading into a colour crescendo of rhododendrons and azaleas. June is awash with the perfume of old-fashioned roses. In July, the walled garden borders are overtaken with colourful perennials, some reaching two metres. Along this walk, which is at the heart of the garden, are three sets of four matching topiary designs of drums, globes and crowns. A stone water basin punctuates this vista.

Don't miss …

» … the rose garden in high summer where a series of arbours are covered with roses and underplanted with catmint and persicaria.

» … delectable fragrant roses such 'Charles de Mills' and 'Constance Spry'. At the end of your visit relax in the café where flowers and herbs are used in teas and cakes.

Best time to visit

This is a garden for all seasons, open all year, even for Christmas lunch. Autumn is the best time for a walk through the arboretum with spectacular autumn leaves of beech, dogwood and tulip trees carpeting the ground. Spring is sensational with wisteria and roses.

Garden details

Handcross, Haywards Heath, West Sussex RH176EB

6.5km S of Horsham

Open mid Feb–Oct, Wed–Sun, 11am–4pm, weekends in winter

Tel +44 (0)1444 400321

www.nationaltrust.org.uk/nymans

Left: 'Rose arbours are under planted with Catmint (Nepeta 'Walkers Blue').
Above: Walled garden walk with one of the four sets of topiary with stone water basins.

21. Sissinghurst

The story of Sissinghurst has been immortalised in books and film. It is considered one of the most influential gardens of the 20th century, the result of the endeavours of Vita Sackville-West and Harold Nicholson, whose controversial Bloomsbury existence still creates intrigue. They worked together in harmony to create one of the most popular gardens ever made.

Timeline: 1930–1957

'These mild gentlemen and women who invade one's garden after putting their silver token into the bowl … are some of the people I most gladly welcome and salute.'
Vita Sackville-West

Description

Just as well Vita Sackville-West thought this way, as the world is in love with her garden! So popular is it that you need a timed ticket in order to limit the number of visitors at any one time. The constraints of Harold Nicholson's design can be clearly observed from the top of the tower, where Vita's exuberant planting can be seen to colour-in between the lines. The two worked well together and their creation has become the benchmark for garden making. Without the structure of the design, the glorious and voluptuous planting scheme would not succeed.

Follow the garden through each room: the Rose Garden; the Herb Garden; Rondelle; Lime Walk; Cottage Garden; Azalea Walk; and the famous White Garden. The use of colour is inspirational throughout: a clematis will share a pillar with a climbing rose and be colour-matched to it; a glorious mix of burnished colours warms the Cottage Garden; and colour explodes in the long Azalea Walk with mollis azaleas on one side and white wisteria on the other.

Don't miss ...

» ... anything. Don't rush this garden, allow a full day to see it all. We advise ringing beforehand to book and try to get in early.

» ... the White Garden and South Cottage.

» ... the tower; all nimble-footed visitors must make the journey up the tower to see the view of the garden and its surroundings from the top. Only this view demonstrates the whole garden design with its circular hedges, axes, vistas and views and if you are lucky in spring, the surrounding golden fields of canola.

Best time to visit

The Broad Walk in spring with mollis azaleas filling the air with scent and wisteria dripping over the walls. June is best for the White Garden with its fabulous white rose arbour (*Rosa mulliganii*) as centrepiece.

Garden details

Sissinghurst, Cranbrook, Kent TN17 2AB

10km E of Goudhurst

Open Mar–Oct, Fri–Tue, 11am–6.30pm (10am, Sat, Sun and bank holidays)

Tel +44 (0)1580 710700

www.nationaltrust.org.uk/sissinghurst

Size 4 hectares

Left: Clematis smothers rosy brick wall.
Right: View from the tower.
Next page left: The tower—worth the climb for the best view of the garden.
Next page right: The Moat walk with Mollis azaleas and white Japanese wisteria (Wisteria longissima).

22. Stourhead

The memory of this landscape will never leave you. It's not a flower garden, it's a magical journey around a huge waterway with exquisite points of interest to capture your attention and focus your view. Stourhead was at the forefront of the 18th-century English landscape movement; a reaction to the formal French style of gardening that was popular at the time. The garden was such a success that Henry Hoare became known as 'Henry the Magnificent'.

Timeline: 1745–1765

Description

Walking around Stourhead with its grottos, temples and lakes is like wandering through a three-dimensional classical landscape painting. We love the maturity of this Arcadian landscape, first planted in 1740 and the majestic trees that furnish it reflected in the lake.

Pavilions anchor Stourhead's magical vistas: the Temple of Flora, the Pantheon, the Corinthian Temple of Apollo, the Pope's Grotto and Turf Bridge. It's a botanical journey too: huge and mature copper beech, exquisite conifers, Handkerchief trees, maples, oaks, ash and elms are here to be appreciated in every season.

The River Stour was dammed to make this enchanting lake and gives the garden its name. As you progress around the lake, each feature builds on the last to make a sublime experience. At the end of the journey you reach a little village with church and inn built by Henry Hoare in the 18th century to accommodate the visitors who, even then, flocked to see the estate. We love this classical masterpiece, Henry Hoare's vision of Paradise.

Don't miss …

» … making a detour down into the Pope's Grotto where you are plunged into darkness. Here in one high-domed chamber lies a reclining statue of Ariadne and in another a river god and water nymph. The earthy smell, filtered light and trickles of water charge the senses, a complete contrast to the world beyond.

» … a rest on the steps of the Temple of Apollo high on a hill with glorious views over gardens.

Best time to visit

Enchanting to visit early on a May morning with the fragrance of azaleas filling the air. Really enjoyable at any time.

Garden details

Stourton, Warminster, Wiltshire BA12 6QD
5km NW of Mere
Open daily 9am–7pm (or dusk if earlier)
Tel +44 (0)1747 841152
www.nationaltrust.org.uk

Left: Temple of Flora.
Above: Temple of Apollo.

23. The Eden Project

After two and half years of construction, and a cool £80 million, the Eden Project opened in March 2001. This series of 21st-century giant biomes, or glasshouses, were built at the bottom of a reclaimed china pit two kilometres from the town of St Blazey in Cornwall. Nothing prepares you for the sight of these three huge bubble-shaped, glass domes emerging from a rural landscape.

Timeline: 2001

Description

Plants are given pride of place here. Founder Tim Smit, the British businessman now famous for his work on Cornwall's 'Lost Gardens of Heligan' and the 'Eden Project', wants to foster humankind's love of plants from all over the world. The humid tropics biome is the largest conservatory in the world and encapsulates the total tropical experience: waterfalls, rainforest, streams and wildlife. Bite-sized pieces of rainforest information are easily digestible so children can better understand resources from this environment. If you can't take your child to a real rainforest, this one will do!

The second biodome is a warm temperate climate and the third a Mediterranean climate. The domes are made out of hundreds of hexagons plus a few pentagons that interconnect the whole construction; each a transparent cushion made of toughened plastic keeps the inclement Cornish weather out and the 'created' climate in.

Don't miss …

» … in the tropical biome, the largest of the biomes, the chance to count the number of economic and edible plants.

» … the rare Wollemi Pine, planted by its discoverer, David Noble.

Best time to visit

Climatically controlled, this garden looks the same every day of the year. Don't be put off if it's a windy day in Cornwall, you will find shelter in the biomes, and peace and quiet!

Garden details

Bodelva, St Austel, Cornwall PL24 2SGE
Open Mar–Oct, 10am–6pm (winter till 4.30pm, closed Christmas Eve and Christmas Day)
Tel +44 (0)1726 811911
www.edenproject.com

Left: Inside the tropical dome of the Eden project.
Above: Tropical and temperate biomes.

24. The Lost Gardens of Heligan

Blanketed by brambles for 70 years, this 17th-century garden was a sleeping beauty until 1987 when four men decided to bring it back to life. Heligan was a self-contained estate of 400 hectares has with 20 indoor and 22 outdoor staff working on a number of farms, brickworks, flour mill, saw mill, brewery, orchards and kitchen garden. In 1898 these gardens were described as some of the most interesting gardens in England. After two world wars the gardens were 'lost' in an impenetrable jungle. They were rediscovered by Tim Smit, John Willis, John Nelson and Robert Pool, who restored them to their former glory.

Timeline: 1600s, restored 1987

Description

Visiting this garden is like stepping back in time to a place where the head gardener reined supreme, growing all the fruit, vegetables, herbs and flowers for the 'big house'. The 1.6-hectare vegetable plot grows 300 old varieties (pre 1900) of fruit and vegetables by traditional methods. Britain's last remaining, 'manure-heated' pineapple pit, built in 1720, is found here, restored to its former glory and consistently providing fruit. In fact, the first crop from the freshly renovated pits was given to Queen Elizabeth II for the celebration of her Golden Wedding Anniversary in 1997. How does it work? Manure pits below ground heat up as they decompose. The heat rises and warms the glasshouse sufficiently to ripen pineapples, along with peaches and melons.

On the other side of the walled vegetable plot is a comprehensive collection of Victorian cut flowers: rainbow-coloured zinnias; delphiniums and foxgloves; and retro classics of coleus, amaranthus and cosmos. The boiler houses, toolsheds, a mushroom room, potting shed (all with very low ceilings) provide a fascinating snapshot of the daily life of the gardeners from the period.

Don't miss …

» ... spectacular groves of mature tree ferns (*Dicksonia antarctica*) in the jungle garden. These arrived as ballast from Australia, apparently lifeless blackened stumps that were thrown overboard at the coast near Truro.

» ... a chat with the friendly and informative staff.

Best time to visit

A visit in spring will see romantic gardens surrounding 'Flora's Green' come alive with a bold blaze of rhododendrons, camellias and magnolias. Sir Joseph Hooker's collection of original rhododendrons from the Himalayas, which were planted between 1847 and 1849, is alive and thriving. The *Magnolia campbellii* is another tree collected by the intrepid plant hunters of the 19th century and is said to be the first of its kind planted in the United Kingdom.

Garden details

Pentewan, St Austell, Cornwall PL26 6EN'
Follow signs towards Mevagissey from the A390 at St Austell
Open daily 10am–6pm, winter until 5pm (closed Christmas Eve and Christmas Day)
Tel +44 (0)1726 845100
www.heligan.com

Left: The peach house and the picking garden.
Above right: The pineapple pits.
Below right: Inside the peach house.

25. West Green House

This garden in Hampshire, just an hour out of London, is the dream project of well-known Australian gardener, Marylyn Abbott, who took on the challenge of a derelict house and garden and restored both when she obtained a 99-year lease from the National Trust. Her creative flair has given birth to a suite of gardens that delight all the senses. This young garden is ever expanding with exciting new additions.

Timeline: 1993–2008

Description

Each garden at West Green House has its own identity unified by Marylyn's signature use of colour. Her creative genius is fully expressed in the potager, a formal garden of flowers and vegetables anchored by globular shapes of standard weigela, lavender, allium, santolina and viburnum. Perennials and bulbs are interspersed with the vegetables and decorative iron fruit cages make strong focal points.

The pint-sized potager, a trademark of Marylyn Abbott's, is juxtaposed by a grand and aristocratic water garden with a grand water staircase that leads the eye to the focal point of the restored Nymphaeum designed in classic style. Beyond is the theatre lawn, an eye-resting green space for performance, with the classic facade of the 18th-century house as backdrop.

The Paradise Garden with water fountains is a cleverly designed new addition and beyond it is the Lake Field with wild garden and restored lake. Another of the delights: a whimsical Alice in Wonderland garden features touches of red in peonies, poppies and garden furniture, where you can enjoy afternoon tea.

Don't miss …

» … the topiary garden beside the house where waterlilies flourish in small water tanks sunk into the ground. The topiary garden runs up to a handsome aviary inhabited by unusual breeds of bantams and chickens.

» … the shop which is a gardener's delight.

» … afternoon/morning tea in the Alice in Wonderland garden.

Best time to visit

Because Marylyn has 15,000 tulips planted every year along with allium and other spring bulbs, the garden bursts into glorious bloom in May. June follows with peonies, then roses and clematis.

Garden details

Hartley Wintney, Bassingstoke, Hook, Hampshire.
RG27 8JB
3km W of Hook
Open Apr–Sept, Wed–Sun, bank holiday Mon, 11am–4.30pm
Tel +44 (0) 1252 844611
www.westgreenhouse.co.uk
Size 4 hectares

Left: The parterre adjacent to the house.
Above: The Alice in Wonderland garden.
Next page left: The potager with alliums in full flower.
Next page right: Allium gigantium.

Ireland, Scotland & Wales

With the influence of the Gulf Stream, gardens in Ireland, Scotland and Wales embrace a large palette of plants and entice garden lovers out of England to the Scottish moors, Welsh hills and picturesque Irish towns. The gardens we love here boast extensive plant collections, spectacular views and a slightly different perspective than those found in England. They range in style from the modern masterpiece at the Garden of Cosmic Speculation, to the more traditional perennial borders of Crathes Castle; from the intimacy of Helen Dillon's garden to the fanfare of Drummond Castle.

Crathes Castle aerial view.

26. Bodnant

Wales's best-known and much-loved garden is located on the north coast of Wales overlooking the Irish Sea 80km south west or one and a quarter hours drive from Liverpool and well worth the four hour drive from London. It's influenced by a warm current of the Gulf Stream, which fosters the cultivation of an extraordinary number of plant species. The garden is highly regarded for its collection of Chinese rhododendrons, which were collected by Henry Pochin in the late 1800s. Bodnant has been a property of the National Trust since 1949.

Timeline: 1875–1949

Description

Perhaps the most copied aspect of this garden is the laburnum tunnel, a 55-metre tunnel of gold when in full flower. The other two favourite highlights are the Pin Mill Terrace and the Dell Walk. The Pin Mill is on the lowest terrace and is named for the 1730 Pin Mill, which was erected on site in 1938. It is reflected in a rectangular pond filled to the brim with waterlilies, making it a glorious sight in summer. The view to the mountains across the valley of the River Conwy, encompasses Snowdonia and the vista changes with the Welsh weather, dramatically adding to the dimension of the garden.

The Dell Walk accompanies a fast-racing stream whose banks are lined with rhododendrons, astilbes, hostas and hydrangeas. This is a lovely walk in spring; the considerable effort required is rewarded by hundreds of magnolias, azaleas and rhododendrons, all colour-matched on a grand scale. This fine scene contributes much to Bodnant's reputation for featuring the finest collection of plants in Britain.

Don't miss …

» … a chance to visit in late spring (early June) when you must take in a walk beneath the 55-metre world-famous laburnum arch, a spectacular tunnel of gold.

Best time to visit

March–late April: Visitors will be enchanted by the magnificence of the camellias, magnolias, daffodils and other spring-flowering bulbs. Early April to the middle of May is the time to see the beautiful collection of rhododendrons. The Japanese and deciduous azaleas are usually at their best in late May and early June for the famous laburnum arch.

Garden details

Tal-y-Cafn Colwyn Bay LL28 5RE

11km S of Llandudno and Colwyn Bay and 11km N of Llanrwst

Open daily 8 Mar–2 Nov, 10am–5pm

Tel +44 (0)1492 650460

www.bodnantgarden.co.uk

Left: The Dell Walk with acid-loving rhododendron and azalea and waterfall.
Above: The Pin Mill pond with water lilies.

27. Crathes Castle

Located just minutes out of Aberdeen is a fairytale castle. Cared for by the National Trust for Scotland since 1951, the 16th-century castle is set against a 20th-century 'Arts and Crafts' garden. The spectacular colour combinations are world class. Owners Sir James and Lady Sybil Burnett were inspired by the writings of Gertrude Jekyll, the famous British garden designer of the late 1800s. They created eight gardens with individual colour combinations of perennial plants in the picturesque style, including a white garden that predates Sissinghurst.

Timeline: castle 1596, 1702, present garden 1950s

Description

There is a magical approach through the woodland to the impressive castle, built in 1553 by Alexander Burnett as the perfect house for his 21 children! Beneath the castle spreads a yew hedge that dates from 1702. The gardens are set against the backdrop of the turreted castle in a series of walled enclosures.

Often described as 'The Sissinghurst of Scotland', this garden also features a tower that dates from the late 1500s, beside which the garden stands. For centuries the tower stood in lonely isolation, protecting the Burnett family and allowing them fine views of the woods and moors. In the 20th century, the gardens were made by Sir James Burnett of Leys.

The gardens unfold in a series of walled enclosures each with a different colour scheme. Pinky-brown stone walls add a lovely background to these colour combinations, along with sculptured topiary and unique planting.

Wander along the herbaceous flower borders and be dazzled by the clever use of colour: the Gold Garden, created in memory of Sir James's wife, Lady Sybil Burnett, features shades of gold, yellow and

lime foliage planted with blue and white flower accents. The White Border is filled with philadelphus, Canterbury bells, roses, hostas, deutzia and astilbe. The Blue Walk has monks hood, double lilacs, geraniums, delphiniums, agapanthus and foxgloves.

Don't miss …

»   … the chance to slowly wander through the soft green pathways winding in and out of the borders, twisting and turning, interrupted by rose-covered arbours, giant thistles and the heady scent of philadelphus.

»   … the collection of Malmaison carnations in the greenhouse (flowering June to August).

Left: Gardens are colour coded.
Above: The gardens are set against the backdrop of the turreted castle.
Next page left: A series of walled enclosures.
Next page right: Paths leading through herbaceous flower borders.

Best time to visit

Late summer: The red, orange, yellows and purples of the upper border reach their peak. Colour is planned to last through to September.

Garden details

6km E of Banchory and 125km SW of Aberdeen
Banchory, Aberdeenshire
24km W of Aberdeen
Open daily 9am–sunset
Tel +44 (0)1330 844525
www.nts.org.uk

28. Garden of Cosmic Speculation

This 21st-century garden, created by architectural critic and commentator Charles Jencks in memory of his late wife, Maggie Keswick, depicts in landscape Jencks' life philosophy. Covering 12 hectares in the Borders region of Scotland, this garden clever, unique and mustn't be missed. It embraces mathematics and science to describe natural phenomenon and, although it's not a plant lover's garden, it's a treat for those who like to be challenged. We think it's beautiful.

Timeline: 1997

'... others are unusual: inventing new waveforms, linear twists and a new grammar of landscape design to bring out the basic elements of nature that recent science has found to underlie the cosmos.'

Charles Jencks

Description

The garden uses nature to celebrate nature, both intellectually and through the senses (including a sense of humour!). A new language of landscape design is created, based on the manipulation of landforms into twists, spirals, waves, optical illusions and sudden surprises. It presents a different view of the universe and will delight all those who are interested in how science and life fit together.

We love the man-made landforms that make up this garden, including the grassy, spiral-shaped Snail Mound, whose tail spirals beautifully into the lake. Jencks has created beautiful forms that play with each other.

Sculptures are set into the landscape and are revealed as you walk around: the Black Hole sculpture explores symbolic and physical relationships; the Universal Cascade encourages visitors to climb through 13 billion years of cosmic history to the top, the future; the DNA Garden depicts the building blocks of life and prompts visitors to think more about science and nature.

Don't miss …

» ... the 'ambiguity' stone. Look out for it in the entrance to the DNA garden.

» ... the lawn spiral into the lake.

» ... be open to a deeper meaning, a new language for all the senses and a new way to understand the universe.

Best time to visit

Looks good every day

Garden details

Portrack House, Portrack, Dumphries DG2 0RW
Open through the Scotland's Gardens Scheme only a few days of the year. Groups should apply in writing to
Charles A. Jencks
PO Box 31627
London W11 3XB
United Kingdom
All donations go to Maggie's Centres
Scottish Charity Number SCO 24414
www.gardensofscotland.org

Left: The Snail Mound.
Above: The reflection.

29. The Dillon Garden

Helen Dillon's garden is a jewel that shines with style, class, design and colour. It is a compact garden in the heart of Dublin, which makes it easy to explore and satisfying to grasp. Because of this personal scale, it's a garden you can relate to and learn from.

Timeline: 1977–2008

'For later life you should plan your garden so that gardening is of the most tranquil kind, with masses of time for sitting and thinking how lovely everything is, without being harassed by urgent gardening chores.'

Helen Dillon

Description

Helen Dillon has spent 30 years creating her garden—an expression of her personality as well as a demonstration of her superb plant selection and clever design. A simple reflective canal at the heart of the garden mirrors the sky and makes a fine balance for the extravagance of the flowery borders either side; hot fiery colours on one side and cool blues on the opposite. The planting is orchestrated with a sequence of continual flower and foliage from late winter through to the senescence of late autumn.

Clever design has made the best possible use of the space. Intimate areas of interest include the statue of the fleeing nymph at the end of the rose tunnel; a wonderful collection of alpines; a sunken terrace with a well-staged collection of potted plants and a series of arbours covered with the rose 'Cornelia' that frame the end of the canal. The canal gives this garden an expansive feeling that belies its size, and the opalescent quality of the Irish light endows each colour of flower and leaf with a luminous quality.

Don't miss …

» … any part of this compact garden. You will enjoy its hidden spaces that offer an opportunity for clever planting schemes.

» … You will enjoy Helen's sense of style and her ruthless philosophy where any plant that doesn't perform at its peak is out and quickly replaced.

Best time to visit

Divine in late spring with roses and poppies and spires of foxgloves and delphiniums stretching their vertical accents.

Garden details

45 Sandford Road, Ranelagh, Dublin 6

Open Mar, Jul, Aug daily 2–6pm; Apr, May, Jun, Sept, Sun only, 2–6pm

Tel +353 (0)1 497 1308

www.dillongarden.com

info@dillongarden.com

Size less than 0.5 hectare

Left: A shady garden set to the side with leafy arbours.
Above right: Lady's mantle (Alchemilla mollis) surrounds a cherub fountain.
Below right: Terracotta urn with Helichysum 'Limelight'.

30. Ilnacullin Gardens

There is no other garden quite like this one, set on its own enchanted island. A short boat trip across Bantry Bay heightens your level of anticipation. Blessed with spectacular sea and mountain scenery as well as a balmy climate brought by the warm waters of the Gulf Stream, this 15-hectares island has a seductive mixture of formal and informal gardens.

Timeline: 1910–1914

Description

Ilnacullin, the 'island of holly', was originally nothing more than a rock covered with heather, surmounted by a Martello tower, when it was purchased in 1910 from the War Office by John Annan Bryce, a Belfast businessman and Scottish MP. Bryce commissioned the English architect and horticulturalist Harold Peto (1854–1933) to design a garden on the island.

From 1911 to 1914, more than 100 were engaged in moving soil, blasting rocks, planting trees, laying paths, as well as building a walled garden, a tall clock tower and a wonderful Italianate garden. Peto's use of Italian Renaissance architecture and his adaptation of the picturesque formal style of gardening, made popular by the famous Lutyens and Jekyll partnership, proved to be brilliantly successful in this island setting, although it was nearly a generation later before his work would be fully appreciated.

The highlight for us is the Italianate casita (tearoom) and arched pavilion that overlooks the classic Italian Garden, a formal sunken garden featuring a reflection pool, urns and colonnade.

Intersecting axes within the garden allow glimpses of the surrounding mountains and seascapes. Elsewhere the garden features oriental touches in twinned pavilions, lichen-covered rocks, drifts of azaleas and plantings of the Japanese umbrella pine and magnolias. The walled kitchen garden features matching iron gates at

each end and is flanked by wide herbaceous borders brimming with varieties of aster, phlox, campanula, dianthus, cornflower, delphinium and erigeron. The garden is warmed by the Gulf Stream, so tender exotics and plants from Australia and New Zealand flourish.

Don't miss …

» … the walk up to the Martello tower, built in 1805 on the highest point of the island as a defence fort. You will have a panoramic view of the entire garden and to the waters of the inlet and the mountains beyond.

» … the grassy walk through Happy Valley to the Grecian temple that overlooks Bantry Bay.

Best time to visit

High summer is lovely when the herbaceous borders reach their peak of flowering.

Garden details

Glengariff, County Cork
Get the private boat from Glengariff
Open daily 1 Mar–31 Oct
Tel +353 (0)27 63007

Left: Walled herbaceous border in full summer flower.
Above: The classic Italian garden.

31. Mount Stewart

In the north of Ireland, 20 minutes from Belfast, lies this grand-scale, impressive sequence of gardens in an idyllic position at the head of the Ards Peninsula with views across Strangford Lough. Exotic luxuriance pampered by the Gulf Stream, a unique microclimate and an entertaining sense of theatre makes this garden deserving of its World Heritage listing.

Timeline: 1785–1955

'Gardens are meant to be lived in and enjoyed and I hope they may long continue to be a source of pleasure to those who visit them ...'

Edith, Lady Londonderry.

Description

The Vane-Tempest-Stewart family bought the 40-hectare estate in 1744 with money acquired by Alexander Stewart. This new wealth came from the sales of materials such as linen. At the time, the house was known as Mount Pleasant. Edith married the 7th Marquess and started to redesign the gardens in the most lavish way possible. When her husband had succeeded to the Marquessate in 1915, the gardens had just been plain lawns with large decorative pots.

Edith, Lady Londonderry added the Shamrock Garden, the Sunken Garden, increased the size of the lake, added a Spanish Garden with a small hut, the Italian Garden, the Dodo Terrace, the Menagerie, the Fountain Pool and laid out walks in the Lily Wood and the rest of the estate. This dramatic change led to the gardens being proposed as a UNESCO World Heritage site. After she created her garden, and after the death of her husband, Edith gave the gardens to the National Trust in 1955.

Her particular whimsy is expressed throughout the Dodo Terrace in particular, which features topiary animal statues and a line of carved monkeys sitting on columns representing politicians of the time. A topiary hunting scene is clipped into the top of a circular hedge, a fox being endlessly chased. There's Irish symbolism in the

Shamrock Garden, where Edith planted yew topiary in the shape of an Irish harp with red begonias to represent the red hand of Ulster.

Join up with the many walks around the estate that take you to the Spanish and Italian parterres and the Sunken Garden, planted in the style of Gertrude Jekyll, and to the other side of the house around a huge lake with a tranquil woodland garden scattered with plenty of benches, magnolias, rhododendrons and dove-tree or handkerchief trees (*Davidia*).

Don't miss …

» … the walk up to the romantic Temple of the Winds for magnificent views across Strangford Lough.

» … the *Magnolia campbellii*, planted in the 1920s and which first flowered on April Fool's Day in 1956. Edith, Lady Londonderry spotted the magnificent bright pink bloom on the highest branch and thought that someone had played a joke on her but, to her delight, it was the first of many blossoms to appear every spring time.

» … the culinary delights in the Bay Restaurant.

Best time to visit

Spring: The woodland garden around the lake is flowering with rhododendrons and azaleas in bloom

Garden details

30km SE Belfast

Portaferry Rd, Newtownards, County Down
 BT22 2AD

Open daily Mar, 10am–4pm; Apr, 10am–6pm;

May–Sept, 10am–8pm; Oct, 10am–6pm

Tel: +44 (0)28 4278 8387

www.nationaltrust.org.uk

Left: Mount Stewart House, pond and plants.
Above: The symmetrical Spanish garden with cobblestone path and summerhouse.

Chapter 3

NORTHERN EUROPE

The complex history of this part of Europe is reflected in the gardens. Kings, queens and emperors built grand gardens as expressions of power. The French Revolution, the rise of Communism and two catastrophic world wars have taken their toll on the culture of Europe. Many devastated landscapes have been and continue to be magnificently restored.

The French style, initiated by André Le Nôtre at Vaux-le-Vicomte and given full expression at Versailles, was much copied all over Europe and still continues today. The English Landscape style became popular in France, Austria, Germany Scandinavia and Russia, as well as in the United Kingdom and the United States, a reaction to the formal French style. Formality was relaxed and a more natural picturesque style became fashionable.

Keukenhof's tulip display.

France

France revels in gardens of kings and kitchens; parterres and perfume; monasteries and modern parks. The triumph of the traditional French garden is formality. The formal French style captured the imagination of gardeners all over the world during the 17th century. After the French Revolution the romantic English Landscape style of Capability Brown and Humphrey Repton became popular as formality was abandoned even in France. In recent times, French gardens have revived this formal old-world style.

In the north of France the climate is good for growing roses, leading to some significant rose gardens such as the Roserie Bagatelle and Roserie Val-de-Marne in Paris. The best time for viewing these gardens is in June. In the south, the climate is great for growing citrus, olives, grapes and geranium and the garden style is 'Mediterranean'. French gardens are an extension of the French celebration of life, so a garden visit can also be an opportunity for gourmands. Vive la France!

Clos Normande, flower gardens leading up to Monet's home.

32. Bagatelle Rose Garden and Potager

Set in the heart of the Bois de Boulogne in Paris is one of the finest rose gardens on the planet. Rose lovers who catch it at its peak of flowering, and the timing is crucial, will be ecstatic. The roserie is famous but there is a beautiful potager for fruits and vegetables growing with style and panache that shouldn't be missed. Thomas Blaikie's park, with exquisite and eccentric 'divertissements' is reason enough for a visit.

Timeline: 1775

Description

One word to describe Bagatelle? *Magnifique!* The whole suite of gardens that make up this glorious park display unmatched horticultural excellence. The rose garden is the masterpiece of the collection. It's formal in style, set beside the miniature chateau and orangery. An elevated pavilion allows you to fully appreciate the spectacle. Climbing roses decorate huge pillars, rope swags and a series of pergolas around the perimeter. There are said to be 10,000 rose plants representing varieties.

We like to enter through the potager or kitchen garden, which has a walled garden as its backdrop, the boundary wall of Bagatelle. Smothered with roses and clematis this garden is breathtakingly beautiful in flower. Further along is a hedged iris garden that you step down into, with a superb range of named varieties of bearded iris, which reach their peak of flower at the end of May, overlapping the roses.

Don't miss …

» … the pretty formal garden in front of the miniature chateau with a fine collection of peonies (be there late May to catch them) and enjoy a stroll through the expansive English style park with majestic trees.

» …the stables, which now house a fine restaurant that serves a great coffee after your visit.

» … the cascadres, grotto, pavilion of love, pyramid and water garden.

» … the long, narrow-walled perennial garden with climbing roses and an ever-changing palette of perennial plants.

Best time to visit

Late May into early June is best for the roses. In general, May is lovely for this garden with iris, peonies and clematis all coming into flower.

Garden details

Parc de Bagatelle, Bois de Boulogne, Route de Sèvres-À-Neuilly et Allée de Longchamp, 75016 Paris, France
Open daily 8.30am–7pm
Tel +33 (0)1 40 71 75 60
www.paris.fr

Left: Orangerie.
Above: Formal design of the roserie with beds edged in box.

33. Domaine de Saint-Jean-de-Beauregard

Just 28 kilometres south of Paris lies a charming French chateau with its walled garden, potager and park is picture-book perfect! The garden was restored to its original 17th-century design from plans found in the archives of the chateau at the beginning of the 20th century and was awarded the status 'Monument Historique' in 1993. Established in 1628 and in private family hands ever since, St-Jean-de-Beauregard is a living monument to 17th-century French life.

Timeline: 1628–2008

Description

The owner of St-Jean-de-Beauregard, Madame de Curel, shares her passion for this garden with her visitors. The old walled garden is big, two hectares in fact, with flower borders planted with perennials suited to their south- or north-facing situation. These borders are divided by box 'buttresses', clipped into shape. Within the confines of the walls are flower beds, each one edged with English box to give them permanent structure.

The best-loved part of this garden is the potager or kitchen garden that grows all the fruit and vegetables used by the house. It is divided into four equal squares, each lined with low espaliered apples and pears and separated by two allées, one of peonies and one of bearded iris. In this potager, vegetables are no less ornamental than flowers.

We love the grape house, which was designed to store individual bunches of grapes in small glass bottles and which stretches the table-grape season to six months a year, culminating in a feast of grapes on Christmas Day. This rare chamber uses a 19th-century method. Each bunch of grapes is preserved in its own bottle with a wax seal. Take a moment to look into the pair of lovely old glasshouses used for growing grapevines, one for white grapes, the other for black.

Don't miss …

» … the enormous dovecote, pigeonnier, one of the largest and oldest in France, a treasure of a building with 4500 nesting boxes.

» … the market days during summer and autumn when produce from the potager is sold to the locals.

» … an autumn event called 'Past and Present Vegetables' that attracts both amateur gardeners and experienced collectors, who come to meet the gardeners, scientists and producers of forgotten or rare fruit. Catch one of the demonstrations of fruit-tree pruning or just wander through the displays of strange fruit and vegetables.

» … tour through the historic chateau and you will find a warm family 'lived in' feeling unlike most of the other châteaux you will visit.

Left: Flower borders with beared iris and allium.
Above: Glasshouse with spring allium

Best time to visit

Early spring: Bulbs flower in the orchard and fruit trees are decked in blossom
Summer: Peonies, then iris and then roses reach their peak of flowering
Autumn: Harvest time when the kitchen garden reaches its crescendo

Garden details

91940 Les Ulis, Domaine Saint-Jean de Beauregard, Ile-de-France.
28km SW Paris
Open daily from mid Mar–mid Nov, 10am-6pm; Sun and public holidays, 2–6pm
Tel +33 (0)1 60 12 00 01
www.domsaintjeanbeauregard.com
Size 2 hectares

34. Jardin du Prieuré Notre-Dame d'Orsan

Set in the eastern end of the Loire Valley, approximately 20 kilometres from Bourges is the restored remnants of the ancient Priory of Notre Dame at Orsan. This clever interpretation of a medieval monastery garden shows impeccable attention to detail in the art of horticulture. Fruits of all types are grown to perfection using traditional horticultural methods and no chemicals, and you can eat what you see in the garden once you get to the restaurant.

Timeline: 2004

Description

Designed by Sonia Lesot and Patrice Taravella and under the watchful eye of Master Gardener Gilles Guillot, a medieval time capsule has been created. There is a great commitment to the past. No detail has been overlooked in this productive garden, which reflects the monastery gardens of the Middle Ages. The extensive range of fruits and vegetables includes some modern varieties, but all are grown using techniques dating from 15th century.

This is where utility and religious symbolism come together. All plant supports, trellis, fences and garden furniture are made from young soft woven stems of chestnut. The ambience is cleverly contrived; calm, simple, monastic and spiritually charged. There are no nails or concrete. The only stone used is that of the remnant priory buildings, which have been restored and rebuilt to house a shop, restaurant and accommodation. The whole design is symbolic: parterres of broad beans and wheat, cloisters of hornbeam hedges and Gothic windows of woven chestnut twigs in the roserie.

Don't miss …

» … anything in this garden. It's all quite magical. Take time to observe the detail. Don't miss the tiny pear growing inside its bottle! See the stones used as weights to train the young pear stems and keep them straight. Watch the butterflies that proliferate in this chemical-free environment.

» … the espaliered apple maze.

Best time to visit

This is a garden for all seasons. In spring, it's alive with almost palpable energy. In summer, the roses bloom and the fruit swells. In autumn, the leaves colour and it's harvest time. You can stay in the hotel onsite to fully appreciate this quite wonderful garden.

Garden details

Le Prieuré d'Orsan

18170 Maisonnaise France

25km W of Saint-Amand-Montrond

Open daily Apr–Oct, 7am–7pm

Tel +33 (0)2 48 56 27 50

www.prieuredorsan.com

Left: Home is where the heart grows.
Above right: Chestnut is woven into decorative structures.
Below left: Stone weights help train the apple branches.
Next page left: Hornbeam cloisters enclose the vineyard.
Next page right: 'Pierre de Ronsard' rose climbs over stone walls of the Priory.

35. Giverny

In the spring of 1883 during his search for a family home, Monet found the town of Giverny 75 kilometres northwest of Paris. Visiting Giverny is like walking into one of Claude Monet's famous paintings. Step through the front gate and you are engulfed in flowers. Stroll through his water garden and it's a watery canvas. Monet captured the remarkable quality of light and expressed it on canvas. His garden was his inspiration. His creative genius was twofold: he designed and planted his garden and then he painted it.

Timeline: 1883–1892

'I perhaps owe being a painter to flowers.'   Claude Monet

Description

There are essentially two gardens here, the flower garden around the house and the water garden or stream on the other side of the road. The contrast between the two is delightful. The Flower Garden (Clos Normande) is a series of parallel flower borders. The Grande Allée is the biggest, covered in a series of giant arches supporting climbing roses that reach their peak of flower in June. The garden here is all about colour, a plot of flowers planted in abundance with varieties chosen for contrasting and complementary harmonies.

The water garden has its roots in the Japanese tradition: a lake, winding paths and points of contemplation. Monet enhanced the oriental tone by planting bamboo, Japanese maples, tree peonies, weeping willows, water iris and waterlilies. The simple curved bridge was built in the Japanese style, but Monet painted it green rather than the traditional red, capped it with a trellis to support wisteria and created an instantly recognisable horticultural icon.

Don't miss …

»   … Monet's pretty pink house with green shutters, which is almost as he left it. It's a lovely background to the garden and is filled with memorabilia that offers an insight into the life and times of Claude Monet.

»   … the apple trees still growing in the garden, which attracted Monet to Giverny in the first place.

»   … the town of Giverny. It's a special place with many sights such as the American Museum of Art with a pretty flower garden.

Best time to visit

Serene early morning with butterflies, bees and wafting fragrance and when mist hangs over the lake. If you arrive early, you will miss the huge crowds that can fill this garden and detract from your experience of it.

Garden Details:

84, Rue Claude Monet, 27620 Giverny, France

2 hr drive NW of Paris

Open daily 1 Apr–31 Oct (except Mon), 9.30am–6pm

The garden closes on 31 Oct for five months for regular winter maintenance.

Tel +33 (0)2 32 51 28 21

www.fondation-monet.com/uk/informations/index

Left: Flower gardens arranged in allees with arbours of roses.
Right: Monet loved iris, almost as much as he loved waterlilies.
Next page left: Japanese bridge in the famous Water Garden.
Next page right: Boatmen keep the water clean.

36. Marqueyssac

This garden overlooks the Dordogne River Valley in the *Périgord* region of France. It is a garden like no other, a garden of 150,000 evergreen boxwood trees, now 100 years old, that have been sculpted into organic abstract and undulating forms. There is nothing rigid or geometric here; it's a gentle, sinuous landscape that links with the landscape.

Timeline: 1866 to present

Description

Its remarkable position on a spur 130 metres above the Dordogne with panoramic views over the entire valley gives this garden its focus.

Six kilometres of pathways (you'll need sturdy shoes!) lead from the Chateau at one end of the spur, through the various spaces, to the Belvedere at the other. This elevated balcony, standing 192 metres above the valley, offers the visitor the best views of the region. The hand-pruned 150,000 evergreen box were planted in the late 19th century in a fluid 'rolling' design of shapes that demonstrates great imagination and grace. This area alongside the chateau is called the Bastion.

Julien Cerval inherited Marqueyssac in 1861. He was a passionate gardener, greatly influenced by Italian culture so he planned this series of terraces he loved in Italy with cypress, linden, laburnum, cercis and umbrella pines. The garden underwent extensive restoration in 1990s and was finally opened to the public in 1997.

Don't miss ...

» ... an ice-cream from the parlour on the panoramic terrace.

» ... the cliff walk past the loggia, chapel, waterwall, Esplanade, toddlers circuit, Pope's Seat and a wayside cross to the belvedere. These features accentuate the natural beauty of the site.

» ... a carriage ride drawn by a huge, calm Percheron mare for those needing a gentle ride back to the entrance.

Best time to visit

Between August and October you will see flowers; a beautiful carpet of miniature cyclamen. We love the candlelight evenings every Thursday in July and August, from 7pm to midnight, but suggest getting there earlier to appreciate the scenery by daylight. Watch the sun set over the Dordogne.

Garden details

Les Jardins de Marqueyssac, 24220 Vezac, France
Open daily, 9am–8pm July and August, 10am–7pm in April, May, June and September.
Tel +33 (0)5 58 31 36 36
www.marqueyssac.com
Size 54 acres

Left: The chateau makes a grand backdrop to topiary.
Above: Fluid hedges roll throughout making this garden unique.

37. Château de Villandry

Set in the picturesque Loire Valley 15 kilometres from Tours lies this World Heritage listed classic potager. This famous vegetable garden is decorated with flowers, within a framework of geometric greenery. The gardens have been restored to match the context of the Renaissance chateau, so they sit together in perfect harmony.

Timeline: Present gardens 1906–1924

Description

Villandry is a magical place with a real sense of purpose. Three terraces make use of the sloping site. The lowest terrace is the most famous. It's a complex set of squares all planted with vegetables, each one a different colour, all edged with box. The entire vegetable-planting scheme is completely changed twice a year –: in March for the spring crop and in June for the summer season. The middle parterre terrace is planted in box with hearts, daggers, masks, fans and music symbols as a series of knot gardens, one terrace symbolising love, the other music.

The garden is outlined in neat pleached hornbeam hedges, clipped topiary yew and miles of interwoven buxus hedge. At the top lies a sheet of water, a mirror lake and a simple counterpoint for the complex parterres on the two lower levels. Water flows from the lake down a series of cascades and into the moat around the chateau.

Don't miss …

» …. climbing the ramparts via a stone staircase within the north wing. From here the intricate design of the parterres can be fully appreciated. Renaissance gardens were designed to be viewed from the upper levels of the residence.

» … the medicinal herb garden and a new perennial garden (where the labyrinth used to be).

» … two wonderful shops, one inside with gifts and one outside with cute French-inspired gardeners' stuff. We can't resist either.

Left: Cabbage and lettuce are planted in large colourful blocks.
Above: A Renaissance chateau provides the walls to the kitchen garden room.
Next page left: Geometrical arrangements of vegetables are edged in box.
Next page right: The Music Garden planted with music symbols.

Best time to visit

The height of summer is lovely with leafy arbours providing welcome shade. Box parterres flower with red, pink and white begonias. Two hours before sunset is a magical time when the light is soft and the evening is cool.

Garden details

Château de Villandry, 37510 Villandry France
15km W of Tours and 250km SW of Paris
Open daily 9am–sunset
Tel +33 (0)2 47 50 02 09
www.chateauvillandry.com

38. Château de Vaux-le-Vicomte

Nestled in the French countryside 55 kilometres southeast of Paris near the town of Melun is the chocolate box Château de Vaux-le-Vicomte. This garden is a classic example of the French formal style, indeed the first by André Le Nôtre. His initiation of this style of garden was much copied all over Europe. A triumph of perspective, broderie parterres spread like a carpet from the chateau to the great canal.

Timeline: 1656–1661, restored 1875

Description

Château de Vaux-le-Vicomte was the epitome of aristocratic taste in 17th-century France. Its charm lies in its vistas, changing levels and enticing cross-axes. The fairytale chateau is set on a platform and surrounded by a moat. The chateau and courtyards, stables, coach house and outbuildings are proportional and integrated in harmony.

The garden's very success was its owner's tragedy. Nicholas Fouquet was Louis XIV's Minister of Finance, but after Louis saw Vaux-le-Vicomte, Fouquet was accused of embezzlement and jailed. Louis employed Fouquet's designers (Le Brun, Le Nôtre and Le Vaux) for his own palace at Versailles and the gardens at Vaux declined. Most of the statues and trees were taken to Versailles.

It was not until 1875 that Alfred Sommelier reconstructed the gardens at Vaux, using the plans of Le Nôtre. Make sure you visit the chateau and enjoy the view of the garden from the upstairs rooms. Many movies have been filmed here including *Marie Antoinette* and *Man in an Iron Mask*.

Don't miss …

»   … a chance to get around in comfort. Because this estate is so enormous, it is worth hiring an electric buggy to take you to the extremities, as far as the statue of Hercules at the end of the grand vista.

»   … the fountain show every second and last Saturday of each month from end March to end October from 3pm to 6pm.

Best time to visit

It's magical to arrive on a Saturday evening in summer as thousands of candles are lit to outline every window, parapet and balustrade of the chateau, every step and pathway of the garden. Book in for dinner to enhance this experience and enjoy a glass of champagne in the garden while the sun sets and the music plays.

Garden details

Seine-et-Marne France
5km E of Melun
Open 15 Mar–9 Nov, 10am–6pm,
closed 10 Nov–19 Dec
Tel +33 (0)1 64 14 41 90
www.vaux-le-vicomte.com

Left: Andre le Notre's masterpiece of perspective.
Above: Formal French-style perfection.

39. Château de Versailles

The grandest garden of all time set a benchmark for kings and queens the world over to imitate but never to match. One hour from the heart of Paris is the town of Versailles and a classic Italianate palace, flower and water parterres, fountains, allées and a huge park to wrap it all up. It was built as a visible symbol of the power of King Louis XIV with gardens designed by André Le Nôtre.

Timeline: 1665—1683, replanted 1775

Description

The gardens of Versailles are almost unimaginably large. The Grand Canal alone is 3.5 kilometres long. It is the main axis at the heart of the landscape and features the Neptune Fountain and the Fountain of Apollo. There are 1400 fountains at Versailles and they flow on Sunday afternoons in summer. While the garden is grand (Le Nôtre flattened hills, drained swamps and planted thousands of trees to create the landscape at Versailles) there are small details that delight. We love the hidden bosquets (an intimate niche within a hedge) featuring an exquisite statue, urn or fountain.

Highlights include the Orangery, where tender trees are over wintered in Versailles planters, the flower-filled parterre gardens on either side of the Palace, the Grand Trianon with the grandest of all flower gardens, and the Petite Trianon built in 1774 as a gift from Louis XV1 for Marie Antoinette. You need two days to see it all and include a visit into the palace, where you will see the significant Hall of Mirrors and the luxurious interiors of the period.

Don't miss …

» … hiring an electric buggy to visit the Hameau (the Hamlet)
with farm, cowshed, dairy, barn, kitchen garden and half-timbered houses with thatched roofs that were used as private apartments where Marie Antoinette could escape formal public life in the palace.

» … Potager du Roi (the Kitchen Garden of the King, built 1677–1683), managed by the School of Horticulture where students will guide you.

» … taking a picnic to enjoy in the garden.

» … hiring a paddleboat on the Grand Canal.

Best time to visit

Best time to visit is any Sunday afternoon in summer when the fountains play and classical music heralds the occasion.

Garden details

Château de Versailles, Versailles 78000 France

25km SW of Paris

Open daily 7am–sunset

Tel +33 (0)1 30 83 78 00

www.chateauversialles.fr

Left: The view to the palace with summer flowers planted in swirling parterres.
Above: The ornamental lawn parterre in front of the Orangery.
Next page left: Orangery with palms, Versailles planters and the circular pool in the height of summer.
Next page right: The Fountain of Latona.

40. Villa Ephrussi de Rothschild

On the Cote d'Azur between Nice and Monaco is Cap Ferrat, where Baronne Béatrice Ephrussi de Rothschild used her wealth to flatten a promontory on this stretch of the Mediterranean coast. She created a series of gardens to echo her extensive travels around the world. It is one of the finest properties on the French Riviera. The estate was bequeathed to the people of France in 1991 through the Académie de Beaux-Arts.

Timeline: 1905–1912

Description

The eccentric palazzo-style pink villa is crammed full of the Baronne's treasures, and the gardens are just as eclectic. Arranged like the decks of a sea-going liner; a sunken Spanish-Moorish garden with classic loggia, a Japanese garden with exotic pagoda, an Exotic garden with impressive cacti, a Provençal Garden and an English Garden in the bottom corner complete with roses: these seven themes gardens surround a formal terrace.

A canal at the heart of the garden links a cascade from a rotunda to the lily pond in front of the villa and forms an axis around which the garden is organised. Head straight for the figure of Venus, with Corinthian columns, which is based on the Temple of Love at Le Petite Trianon at Versailles. Here you will find the best picture postcard view of the villa and garden. We love the Florentine terrace with balustrades and double sweeping 'horseshoe' staircase. There are spectacular views from every part of the garden over the Mediterranean Sea.

Don't miss …

» … the villa itself, now the Rothschild Museum, with priceless antique furniture, paintings and porcelain. Views of the garden from the windows show how closely the garden relates to the villa.

» … tea in the café inside the villa.

Best time to visit

The gardens are lovely at sunset when the fragrance of jasmine and exotic plants fills the air.

Left: Gardens are set on a flattened spur with spectacular views of the Cote d'Azur.
Above: Water gardens, palms and bedding begonias lend an exotic charm to the gardens.
Next page left: Italianate pink stucco villa reflects in the central canal.
Next page right: Views from the Villa's veranda are not to be missed.

Garden details

Villa Ephrussi de Rothschild
St-Jean-Cap-Ferrat 06230 France
Open daily 10am–6pm (7pm Jul–Aug). Closed winter weekday mornings
Tel +33 (0)4 93 01 33 09
www.villa-ephrussi.com

41. Val Joanis

Set in the middle of the Provençal landscape a short drive from Aix-en-Provence is the vineyard and olive grove of Val Joannis. The garden of Cécile Chancel is a modern terraced garden. Italian visitors think there are too many flowers and the English think there are not enough! We think the garden is a sensible mix of edible vegetables and beautiful flowers, surrounded by a delectable mix of vines and olives.

Timeline: 1990

'Gardens are like husbands — you can't have two at a time.' Cécile Chancel

Description

We noticed a golden theme during our visit on a sunny summer afternoon with burnished orange roses 'Christopher Columbus', golden yellow yarrow and bright tangerine pokers. This is the only vineyard in France with such spectacular gardens. Go directly to the cellar door for entry through to the garden.

While in the garden you will be interested in the symmetry of elegant Italian cypress planted along lines of lavender set against delicious flowers and vegetables. Espaliered apples 'Golden Hornets' are trained to create living fences. We love the domestic scale of the garden art, pieces that we would put in our own gardens such as scarecrows, bird boxes, snail sculptures, entwined branches, timber pots with cute metal hats, woven willow cages and watering cans.

Don't miss …

» … sitting beneath the boughs of the plane trees in the courtyard for a lazy afternoon tasting Val Joanis wines.
» … a tour of the winery.

Best time to visit

Summer's display of lavender, orange roses, yellow yarrow, tomatoes and roses seems as hot as the Provençal landscape.

Garden details

Val Joanis, Pertuis 84120 France

Open daily 9am–5pm

Tel +33 (0)4 90 79 20 77

www.val-joanis.com

Left: Artistic garden sculptures personalise this garden.
Right above: Quaint garden cottage.
Below: Pokers and yarrow are the bold flowers of summer.
Right below: The garden is dotted with topiary, cypress and surrounded by olives and grapes.

42. Jardin Exotique de Monte Carlo

The garden is situated high on a cliff top on the edge of the principality of Monaco with spectacular panoramic views of Monte Carlo Harbour and the French and Italian rivieras. Here you'll find the biggest and best collection of cacti and succulents in Europe. And we think the most beautiful succulent garden in the world. Lovers of dry land plants will be mesmerised by the diversity of foliage forms, thorns, patterns and intricate botanical detail. Take your macro lens with you!

Timeline: 1933 (cactus collected 1895 and moved)

Description

There are 6000 cacti and succulents in this collection. We especially love the groupings of 'Golden Barrel' cacti, the largest collection in Europe. They are said to be 120 years old and the heads measures more than a metre. Their golden glow and lines of spines grow in large clumps, spilling over rock walls. Remember to bubble wrap the kids!

There's a great collection of agaves, which include rare species. Triffid-like plantings of cereus through the garden give height and a surreal Mexican desert feel. A stand of massive elephant foot trees also known as pony tail palms, is a surprise welcome at the entrance of the garden, their swollen trunks measuring more than a metre across.

This is a well-maintained and full succulent garden that may not appeal to all tastes, but the location and panoramic views offer distractions for those who don't find these plants set their hearts singing.

Don't miss …

»   … making the effort to descend the steps into the garden for more surprises.

Best time to visit

Anytime, but a winter visit features the aloe and crassula in flower.

Garden details

Jardin Exotique de Monte Carlo

62 Bvd du Jardin Exotique MC-98002, Monaco

Open daily 9am–6pm to 7pm mid May–mid Sept;

closed 19 Nov, 25 Dec

Tel +33 (377) 93 15 29 80

Size 1.2 hectares

Left: Awesome views of the palace at Monaco-Ville.
Right above: 120-year-old golden barrel cactus.
Below: Pathways lead through the garden's more prickly characters.
Right below: Sculptural aloes.

43. La Roseraie du Val-de-Marne

Jules Gravereaux bought a plot of land in L'Haÿ just 50 kilometers south of Paris, in 1844 and asked Édouard André to design a garden of roses. This garden in the village of L'Haÿ became so popular that the village asked to have its name changed to L'Haÿ-les-Roses. An easy train journey from Paris.

Timeline: 1899

Description

This garden displays the rose in all its forms. There are 13 formal sectors, with 13,100 roses featuring 3200 species and varieties. It's the first ever garden dedicated exclusively to roses; exuberant, joyful, fragrant and triumphant.

This is a conservatory of old roses, which acts as a living library to preserve old varieties – every rose lover's dream. We love the famous ornamental trellis that runs along the rose theatre, covered in the glorious rambler 'Alexandre Girault'. The beds, arbours, pillars, walks and tunnels are edged in box plants, which lend a structure to this otherwise flowery garden and contain its exuberance of form and the profusion of colour.

The garden demonstrates the many techniques of rose growing. Roses are classified according to their type, so you can follow the progression of botanic classes. If you time your visit well (and you understand the French language) you can take part in workshops about growing and propagating roses.

Don't miss …

» …the modern roses on one side of the garden, the formal rose garden with a reflecting pool in the centre and old 'heritage' roses and classic roses on the other side.

» … *glace fraise* (strawberry ice cream) in the kiosk.

Best time to visit

Plan your visit for the month of June, when roses are flowering.

Garden details

The Roseraie of Val-de-Marne, Rue Albert Watel, 94240 l'Haÿ-les-Roses France
Open 7 May–21 Sept 10am to 8pm
Tel +33 (0)1 47 40 04 04
www.roseraieduvaldemarne.fr

Left: Arches of climbing roses.
Above: Rosa 'Alexandre Girault' covers the trellis.

44. Les Jardins du Manoir d'Eyrignac

This garden, in the heart of the Black Périgord is in the region of the Dordogne River Valley, a few hours drive east of Bordeaux and 13 kilometres northeast of Sarlat. The estate has been handed down through *22* generations for the past 500 years. The garden was built as a theatre stage around a 17th-century manor house. Topiary lovers will be amazed by the 4 hectares of immaculate green sculpture.

Timeline: 1700, present gardens 1960

Description

Clipped to within an inch of its life, this garden is carefully pruned and trimmed to achieve its accurate and intricate topiary designs. This greatly appeals to us – as long as we don't have to clip it! We love the 100-metre avenue of interlaced yew, box and hornbeam with a geometric design that lies at the heart of this garden. Specialist topiary trimmers are on hand during periods of peak growth.

Classical and romantic influences of the clipped box and fountains complement the Manor House. The French Garden, with its arabesques of dwarf box, is designed to be seen from the first floor of the manor, a view appreciated only by the residents, as this is a private garden. The newly planted Rose Garden gives the whole garden a touch of romance, lightness and poetry with its fusion of fountain and flowers.

The mirror lake contrasts well against the complexity of the garden; a rest for the eye! The double avenue of yew hedges has 10 pairs of vases set into half-moon alcoves.

Don't miss …

»   … the café where you can let it all sink in.
»   … the garden shop full of exquisite garden accessories.

Best time to visit

We love it anytime, even in winter with the snow blanketing the topiary sculptures and outlining the sculptures in shades of white.

Garden details

Les Jardins du Manoir d'Eyrignac, 24590 Salignac France

13km NE of Salat

Open 1 Jan–31 Mar, 10.30–dusk; 1 Apr–30 Apr, 10am–7pm; 1 May–13 July, 9.30am–7pm; 14 July–20 Aug, 9.30am–dusk; 21 Aug–30 Sept, 9.30am–7pm; 1 Oct–31 Dec, 10.30am–dusk

Tel +33 (0)5 53 28 99 71

www.eyrignac.com   Size 4 hectares

Left: View through the archway to the Romanesque tower.
Above: The grand avenue.
Above right: The avenue of vases and handsomely shaped topiary.
Below right: Rosa 'Crocus Rose'

Germany, Austria & The Netherlands

This area of Europe suffered perhaps the worst devastations of World War II. The Nazis were responsible for a lot of the damage to the cultural landscape. Coupled with the effects of Communism, the damage has resulted in huge gaps in the horticultural record. The gardens we've chosen here have historic value, mostly with royal connections and have been significantly restored.

Picture-postcard views of tulips and pastoral landscapes makes travelling through this countryside scenic and enjoyable. Our tours explore Eastern Europe and we base ourselves in Budapest, Dresden, Prague and Berlin to see landscapes that are being restored since the fall of the Iron Curtain. We have become fascinated with this part of Europe.

A mix of jonquils and tulips.

45. Sansoussi

The groundbreaking garden of Friedrich the Great, built in 1744 at Potsdam, just outside Berlin, is often described as the 'Prussian Versailles'. It was later reworked as a romantic landscape in the English style by Peter Lenne in 1822. It's the most famous garden in Germany. Surviving from the original garden are two treasures: the six vineyard terraces and the Chinese Teahouse. The collection of palaces, gardens and follies is now UNESCO World Heritage listed.

Timeline: 1715–1913, extended 1826, 1860

Description

This is a remarkable landscape, memorable for its diversity and detail and unforgettable for its grand scale. Allow a full day to see it all and start with a guided tour of the palace to give a sense of how everything fits in. From here, head out into the garden, armed with a map, and sturdy shoes (even roller blades!). Distances of up to 4 kilometres are common to reach the outer extremities of the park.

The first sight you see will be the Great Fountain with classical statues and a lovely flower garden surrounding it. Now you need to decide your route. We suggest walking down the terraced vineyard, the signature of Sansoussi, where six huge concave terraces catch the sun. Vines are trained along the walls, studded with 168 niches, each with a fig tree and glazed screens for weather protection.

The axis from the fountain extends into a grand avenue, formed of four rows of lime trees, which lies along the main east-west axis across Sansoussi Park. Many smaller allées, all lined with lime trees, lead from the main axis to other surprising focal points along the way, including follies and palaces. We love the baroque and rococo elements and exquisite architectural features: the Chinese Pavilion with its

mix of rococo and Chinoiserie style; the Temple of Friendship; the Dragon House in Chinoiserie style; the trellised gazebo at the Sansoussi Palace and the Corinthian colonnade that encloses the Court of Honour at the entrance front of the palace.

Don't miss …

» … taking a map with you as this park is enormous.

» … the Sicilian Garden planted with subtropical exotics.

» … the cool Nordic Garden.

» … hiring a bicycle if that takes your fancy!

Best time to visit

Avoid the heat of summer, visit spring or autumn.

Garden details

Park Sanssouci, 14469 Potsdam, Germany
Open 1 Apr–31 Oct, 9am–5pm; 1 Nov–31 Mar, 9am–6pm; closed Mondays
Tel +49 (0)331 9 69 41 90

Left: The Great Fountain circled with classical statues.
Above: The palace sits proud above the terraced vineyard.

46. Karl Foerster Garden

Not far from Sansoussi, also in Potsdam, lies the revolutionary garden of Karl Foerster, the father of contemporary German landscape design and a famous breeder of perennial plants (1874–1970). It's here that Foerster broke with tradition by using the form and texture of grasses interspersed among the colour of perennials to provide year-round interest in the garden. This new style and renewed plant palette changed the face of garden design forever.

Timeline: 1910–present

Description

This domestic and intimate garden showcases Foerster's breeding of 650 new flower varieties and his plant combinations. It is a protected monument, restored and preserved with the help of his granddaughter, Marianne Foerster, who shares his vision.

We love the sense of history in this garden, now celebrating its centenary, and the feeling that Karl Foerster himself is lingering somewhere. His old garden boots are at the front door, planted with succulents. It's easy to find your way through a sequence of garden spaces planted around his home. There's an intimacy in the garden, with loose informal arrangements of plants and romantic dynamic drifts of planting that utilise colour, texture and movement for effect.

Most famous is the sunken garden, where terraces are ranged around a central pond and are spectacularly detailed with plants. This is where Foerster experimented with plants and plant combinations and it remains a place of pilgrimage for garden lovers.

Don't miss …

» … the intensive planting scheme and Karl Foerster's signature plants, *Calamagrostis* 'Karl Foerster' and *Helenium* 'Konigstiger'.

Best time to visit

Lovely all year round, but especially in May when roses, allium, tulips and kolkwitzia are all flowering.

Garden details

Write to: Karl Foerster Garden

Im Raubfang 6, 14460 Potsdam, Germany

Left: Steps lead into the Sunken Garden, where Karl Foerster experimented with plants.
Above: Complex plant combinations with foliage, flowers, colour, texture and movement, make this garden the object of a plant lover's pilgrimage.
Right: Giant alliums feature in spring.

47. Pillnitz

Enjoy a two-hour scenic journey via paddle steamer from Dresden along the River Elbe to the wharf at Pillnitz to visit this baroque garden and rococo palace. This was the summer residence of the kings of Saxony, built from 1706. August the Strong used this garden as a playground and amusement park during the baroque period, and the heart of this garden remains unchanged.

Timeline: 1578, 1706–1826

Description

We love the elegant complex of palaces here. The River Palace was built in baroque-Chinese style in the early 18th century with a formal Pleasure Garden that has been reworked since 1706. The heart of the garden is the grand parterre with fountains and richly planted with roses and bedding plants. The New Palace was an extension built in 1826 to connect the River Palace to the Mountain Palace.

A dramatic avenue of linden and chestnuts forms an axis through the park from the Pleasure Garden, to the statue of Flora. The tranquil English Garden has a pretty domed pavilion built in Italian style and its own lake with an island and decorative bird aviary. It's a gentle and romantic corner of this huge park.

Also worth seeing are the huge Palm House, built in 1859; the large orangerie that over-winters tender plants; and the exquisite Chinese Pavilion.

Don't miss …

» … the ancient camellia, brought from Kew Gardens in England in 1779, the largest and oldest in Europe, kept alive by encasing it in a portable glasshouse every winter. In a good year, it blooms with 30,000 flowers.

Best time to visit

Time your visit for late April to catch the fragrant lilacs in the Lilac Court and the flowering of the ancient camellia. High summer is peak flowering for the parterre, richly planted with colourful bedding plants and roses.

Garden details

Schloss Pillnitz, 1326, Dresden, Germany
Pillnitz is located on the northern side of the River Elbe
13km SE of Dresden.
Open daily 8am–dusk
Tel +49 (0)351 2 61 32 60
www.schloesser-dresden.de
Size 23 hectares

Left: Grand parterre garden with fountain forms part of the Pleasure Garden in front of the River Palace.
Above: Summer bedding plants and roses are well maintained.

48. Keukenhof

One hour south of Amsterdam lies a 28-hectare showcase for the Dutch flower industry. Keukenhof means 'kitchen' gardens, a clue to its origins. But don't be misled, there is nothing domestic about the scale of this enterprise. For nine weeks every spring, these famous gardens draw more than three quarters of a million visitors to see a display of more than seven million flowers, including 1000 varieties of tulips.

Timeline: Setting 1840, bulbs 1949

Description

The informal English landscape-style park dates from 1840 when the straight lines and formality of the former kitchen gardens were abandoned, the estate was planted with trees and a huge lake was created. The lake is a soothing counterpoint in spring when spectacular drifts of tulips, crocuses and daffodils, planted in great blocks of colour, burst into glorious bloom.

The festival gardens are style rooms, sources of inspiration to visitors, encouraging them to experiment with flowering bulbs at home. You can visit pavilions with living rooms designed with typical Dutch cosiness, which demonstrate the use of potted flowering bulbs indoors.

For the duration of the festival there is a changing program of flower exhibitions: amaryllis, freesias, hyacinths, tulips, chrysanthemums, iris, roses, sweet pea, alstroemeria, daffodils, gerberas, lisianthus, African violets, bouvardia, kalanchoe, carnations, asters and hydrangeas. These indoor exhibitions change weekly; there is always a different flower in focus.

Don't miss …

» … a guided free tour scheduled daily at 2pm.

» … the annual Flower Parade, held in late April (the exact date changes each year) with large floats, marching bands and decorated vehicles. The parade travels 40 kilometres through the bulb region from Noordwijk to Haarlem.

Best time to visit

For nine weeks from late March to late May with peak flowering late April.

Garden details

Stationsweg 166a 2161 AM Lisse, The Netherlands

Highway 206 to Lisse in South Holland, one hour from Amsterdam.

Take the direct bus to Keukenhof from Schiphol, The Hague, Leiden and Haarlem.

Open daily late March–mid May, 8am–7.30 pm

Tel +31 (0)252 465 555

www.keukenhof.nl

Size 28 hectares

Left: Tulips make up the bulk of the display.
Above right: Visitors flock between April and early May.
Right: Large areas of bulbs are offset with natural ponds in a park setting.
Next page left: Seven million bulbs including 7,000 tulips varieties are planting each year.
Next page right: Rivers of grape hyacinths are edged with white daffodils.

49. Schonbrun Palace

This is Austria's royal garden, a short and enjoyable trip via metro from Vienna city. Now listed by UNESCO as a World Heritage site, it was commenced in 1698 by the Hapsburg Emperor Leopold 1. His intention was to eclipse in splendour, the Versailles Palace of his rival Louis XIV and to reflect Hapsburg Imperial power. This garden is based on one grand vista from the palace across an enormous formal parterre to the Neptune Fountain and Gloriette.

Timeline: 1698

Description

Start at the arched Gloriette on the horizon of the garden, have a coffee and drink in the panorama from this viewing platform. The Gloriette was an addition by Maria Theresa in 1740 when she ascended the Hapsburg throne. From here you can see the unity and harmony of the palace and its gardens. The great parterre, elaborate in true baroque style, is a reflection of the ornate interior of the palace. This formal 'broderie' has symmetrical patterns of box designs in-filled with coloured stone, flowers and sand. At the time of our last visit, gardeners were planting out violas and geraniums and placing potted standard lantanas into position. The grand Neptune Fountain at the foot of the Gloriette is another embellishment by Maria Theresa.

To one side are the spectacular 19th-century glasshouses, now restored following severe damage during World War II, and full of botanical treasures. The Great Palm House, built in 1880, is a particularly impressive. Made of iron and glass it's divided into chambers that echo different climatic zones. A revolutionary steam-heating system facilitates the cultivation of rare plants and, on our visit, a spectacular display of hydrangeas.

The long central garden axis features branching allées of clipped linden trees and bosquets that embrace classic statues. Tall hedges with classic statues flank the grand parterre.

Don't miss …

» … a guided tour of the palace, well worthwhile to see the splendid interiors in the flamboyant rococo style and to understand the life and times of Maria Theresa.

» … the Privy Garden has been restored with a series of trellised pavilions and fretwork arcades of Virginia creeper. Tender potted plants of citrus and lantana are set out in warm seasons.

Left: Appreciate the harmony and balance of this landscape, climb to the Gloriette for a panoramic perspective.
Above: Begin your visit at the Gloriette.

Best time to visit

Best in summer when the parterre is planted out with colourful bedding plants and evening open-air classic music concerts are scheduled.

Garden details

Schonbrunner Schloss-Strasse Vienna 1130 Austria

Open Schonbrun Palace 1 Apr–30 Jun, 8.30am–5pm; 1 Jul–31 Aug, 8.30am–6pm; 1 Sept–31 Oct, 8.30am–5pm; 1 Nov–31 Mar, 8.30am–4.30pm
Privy Garden 15 Mar–30 Jun, 9am–5pm; 1 Jul–31 Aug, 9am–6pm;
1 Sept–31 Oct, 9am–5pm
Tel +43 (0)1 877 50 87

Scandinavia

Forests of white-trunked birch glisten against vivid green pastures spotted with white clover. Travelling through the Scandinavian countryside during summer is breathtaking. You can visit the aristocratic gardens of royalty or pass by the humble allotment gardens where fruit and flowers mingle.

Sweden during the 17th century was the greatest power in northern Europe. Queen Christina reigned from 1640 to 1654. Her gardens at Drottningholm were set out in the formal French style. As in many parts of Europe, the English landscape style was introduced, first into Drottningholm and Hagapark in Stockholm around 1780. This forever changed the style of Scandinavian gardens. Sweden and Denmark both have royal, aristocratic and historic gardens and all the Scandinavian countries boast lovely park gardens. Nordic countries have long been at the cutting edge of contemporary design and this is reflected in the design of public open-air spaces.

Scandinavians make the most of every minute of their beautiful but brief summer.

50. Fredensborg Palace

It's a fairytale: a girl from Tasmania falls in love with a prince and moves to Denmark to live happily ever after in his kingdom. This is her home, Fredensborg Palace, just north of Copenhagen. Mary and Frederik's wing, Chancellery House, is a rather plain, single-storey, unadorned building; no garden, just a sheet of lawn where the children can play.

Timeline: 1720

Description

This has been the favourite residence of the Danish royal family since it was built in 1720. The formal French gardens were later converted in part to romantic landscape style. Apart from the periods when the royal family is in residence, the gardens are open to the public. The palace itself is grand, built in Italianate style, white with a cupola-style roof.

We love the vegetable garden best of all. It is a favourite too of Prince Henrik, father of Prince Frederik. It's very decorative, with an arbour of roses its full length and cut-flower beds interspersed with vegetable plots. Huge racks have been placed over the empty beds with onions and garlic drying. This garden provides vegetables, fruits and herbs for the palace. Grapes are also planted and produce a small amount of wine. A new orangery faces this garden and is reflected in a mirror pond in front. It's a home for fruiting figs and citrus, but its main use is for functions.

The Reserved Gardens, in French baroque and English-inspired romantic style are the private gardens of the royal family and are usually open to the public in July when the family is not in residence.

Don't miss …

» … the 70 sculptures of Norwegian and Faroese farmers and fishermen that record the cultural history of the people of the time, their dress and tools carved with intricate detail of decoration.

» … the kitchen gardens in July, which supply fresh vegetables for the royal household, and a modern orangery.

Best time to visit

High summer: The herb garden and roses are at their peak

Left: The formal potager lies at the heart of the garden, fully productive all year round.
Above: A formal French parterre makes up part of the royal private garden.

Garden details

Fredensborg Palace,
Slottet 9, DK-3480 Fredensborg, Frederiksborg,
North Zealand, Denmark

Open: Reserved Gardens daily 1–31 July, 9am–5pm. During the same period guided tours of the Orangery and Herb Garden are conducted every 20 minutes from 1–4:20pm. The public areas are always open. In July when the royal family is not in residence, you can take a guided tour of the palace, the reserved gardens, the orangery and the vegetable gardens.
Tel +46 (0)42 13 74 00
www.ses.dk/fredensborgpalace

51. Sofiero Castle

In 1864, Crown Prince Oscar and his wife Sophia bought Skabelycke Farm, just north of Helsingborg overlooking the stretch of water between Denmark and Sweden, in order to build a summer residence. In 1905, when the Swedish-Norwegian union was dissolved, Oscar II gave the palace as a wedding gift to his eldest grandchild, Prince Gustaf Adolf and his wife Margareta. It quickly became the great passion of Gustaf.

Timeline: 1864

Description

It is Gustaf VI Adolf's collection of rhododendrons in particular that has given the Sofiero gardens its fame, although all the gardens are lovely. Crown Princess Margareta died in early 1920 and Crown Prince Gustaf Adolf married Lady Louise Mountbatten who shared Margareta's love of the gardens.

We love the Wall Flowerbed, in shades of primrose, lemon, crimson, pink and lilac, which lies inside the front boundary wall and runs its entire length. Big blocks of colour make this extremely long border particularly impressive. Translucent petals of golden rod, purple liatris and hazy clouds of dusky pink eupatorium and a showy display of hollyhocks are delightful. Maja's Garden for children is a treasure with its playhouse and life-sized dolls, its miniature potting shed, its tiny pea-covered arbours and its pretty vegetable garden.

Don't miss ...

»   ... Margareta's Jubilee Garden, a full-curved garden with masses of blue and white hydrangeas, rose-pink astilbe, lime-green sedum, feathery grasses and violet verbena, full, flowery and feminine.

» ... the Pleasure Garden, a formal garden planted with a romantic mixture of colourful flowers, including violet verbena, mauve heliotrope, pink foxgloves, feathery grasses, crimson carnations, whispy pink gaura and white gypsophila. Quirky topiary shapes – a hen, a duck and a fish – enliven this garden.

» ... the Rose Walk, via the Kitchen Garden, the vinery (where vines from the original plantings still bear fruit) and a really inspirational children's garden, and one of the best dahlia gardens we have ever seen, spied through windows in a hedge of linden.

» ... art exhibitions and open-air concerts in summer.

» ... lunch in the castle restaurant.

Best time to visit

Late May–early June: See the rhododendron display

August: During high summer, see the phlox, dahlias, salvia, nasturtium and hollyhocks in full flower

Late August: Garden Festival

Garden details

Sofiero Castle

Sofiero Slott och Slottspark

S-25189 Helsingborg, Sweden

Opening for the castle is 5 May–5 Oct, 10am–6pm; the park is open throughout the year for walks

Tel +46 (0)42 13 74 00

www.sofiero.helsingborg.se

sofiero@stad.helsingborg.se

Left: Design of the Pleasure Garden is outlined in boxes, giving structure to the chaotic mix of annual and perennial flowers.
Above right: The red-hot border is alive with nicotiana, impatiens, marigolds and petunia.
Below right: Red nasturtiums are planted in long borders.

Russia

In the 18th century remarkable progress was made in Russia due to the driving force of Peter the Great, who was deeply interested in the art of park and garden design. His frequent visits to Europe particularly to the Netherlands had a dramatic influence on his ability to design Russia's new landscape. He engaged European architects to create new gardens and to train Russians. He was particularly taken with the French formal landscape style and this is evident in the landscape design of Peterhof. There are no private gardens of the middle classes left in Russia as these were all wiped out by the Communists. As a consequence, the only gardens to have survived are royal gardens and parks, which have been recreated. To their great credit, the Russians have rebuilt their grand palaces that were virtually destroyed in World War II and opened them to the public.

We have only recently started taking tours to Russia and have been fascinated by St Petersburg. The harsh winter climate limits travelling to spring and summer. We enjoy the pearly opalescent night sky where darkness is denied.

Peterhof, the grandest of water gardens built by Peter the Great as an expression of power.

52. Peterhof

Peterhof was the supreme symbol of the royal power of Peter the Great. The great city of St Petersburg was his grand attempt to 'Westernise' Russia. Peterhof was a celebration of Russian achievement, another garden built to rival Versailles. The palace and park ensemble is World Heritage listed by UNESCO.

Timeline: 1714

Description

Take the hydrofoil across the Gulf of Finland from the Hermitage to the jetty at Peterhof. Your first glimpse will be gilded spires and fountains of the main cascade illuminated by the morning sun. The Great Palace was remodelled by Rastrelli in 1747–54. Its gilded cupolas, silver-tinted roof and 300-metre facade serve as a pedestal for the palace and overlook the grand cascade.

This is the grandest of water gardens. It's built on a steep slope with deep grottoes and marble cascades decorated with statues and fountains. A long canal, acting as the central axis of the garden, opens into the Gulf of Finland. It's a triumph of hydraulic engineering to keep 170 fountains flowing.

The lower park features allées and bosquets decorated with more fountains. We love the vitality, the impression of victory and power. This is encapsulated in the water pouring from the cascade into a central basin featuring an imposing sculpture of Sampson and the Lion, symbolic of Peter's victory over Charles X11 of Sweden. The wealth of gold, the vivid expression of architecture, the power and roar of falling water, create a majestic effect you won't quickly forget.

Don't miss …

» … a walk through the Lower Park; it's a gem with quirky fountains, cascades and a formal baroque garden.

» … Montplaisir, a small palace richly decorated and Peter's favourite, as well as its adjacent Bath House.

» … a stop for coffee in the Orangerie.

Best time to visit

Any morning from May to October when the fountains are flowing (they start at 11am)

Garden details

Peterhof State-Museum Reserve

198516, St. Petersburg ul. Razvodnaya

Open daily 11am–6pm (except Mon and the last Tues of each month)

Tel +7 812 427 7425

www.peterhof.org

Left: Arrive by hydrofoil and see the formal Baroque gardens first.
Above: Guilded statues of the main cascade.
Right: Eclectic mix of flowers and fountains of the lower garden.

53. Pavlovsk

Acknowledged as one of the greatest landscape achievements in Russia, Pavlovsk was gifted by Empress Catherine II to her son Paul. Just an hour out of St Petersburg, the exquisite Palladian-inspired palace, designed by Scottish architect Charles Cameron in 1780, remains the focal point within the landscape of a romantic, English-style park.

Timeline: 1780

'All of Pavlovsk in its entirety constitutes an enormous and integrated poetic world and not for nothing is one pillar on the edge of the park called "the end of the world".'

Mikhail Alpatov (art historian)

Description

The whole landscape at Pavlovsk, with its complex of classic elements, is quite ethereal. The Doric Temple of Friendship, a rotunda that stands on a peninsula beside the Slavyanka River, is skilfully integrated into its surroundings. The Three Graces Pavilion, an open, square, Ionic portico, with three exquisite figures sculptured in marble, overlooks an exuberant formal garden of roses. The Apollo Colonnade was once a circle of Doric columns with an Apollo Belvedere statue, part of which collapsed and left a picturesque ruin. A river winds through this romantic landscape and provides the setting for a succession of vignettes.

There is a pastoral quality to the landscape with white birch-wooded hills, rocky cliffs and an old mill-pond. This succession of romantic scenes integrates perfectly with classical buildings and magnificent sculpture. The sumptuous neo-classical interior of the palace has been faithfully restored after it was almost completely destroyed during the German occupation.

Don't miss …

»   … crossing any one of the fine bridges for the best view of the palace. Here you will find Cameron's Cold Baths and the Apollo Colonnade.

»   … taking a picnic lunch and enjoy the park.

Best time to visit

Lovely in spring and summer. Early morning is best.

Garden details

9 Revolyutsii Str

20 189623 Pavlovsk

30km S of St Petersburg

The palace opening hours are 10am–5pm, closed Fri and the first Mon of each month; the park is open until late.

Tel +7 812 470 2156

www.pavlovsk.org

Left: The Apollo Colonnade, now a picturesque ruin, is worth seeking out in the romantic landscape.
Above: Classic bridge over Slavyanka River gives the best view of the palace.

54. Catherine Park and Palace

The Romanov Tsars established not one but two suburban estates—at Tsarskoe Selo and Peterhof—that, in terms of grandeur and excess, outstrip even Versailles. Tsarskoe Selo lies just outside St Petersburg, a huge landscape and Palladian complex comprising Catherine Palace and Alexander Palace, pavilions, follies and huge expanses of parklands designed in the romantic English landscape style.

Timeline: 1741–1761, restored after World War II

'In Russia we have not summer and winter, but only a white winter and a green winter'
Catharine II

Description

Catherine the Great had a huge admiration for English culture and changed the original formal French style park surrounding her palace into the romantic English landscape style. Enchanting architectural features, rotunda, obelisk, bridges and even a Chinese village adorn the landscape. We know how much this palace and its park meant to Catherine; it was her refuge from court life in the city. In the neoclassic Cameron Gallery, a glazed, covered walkway with an impressive double staircase, Catherine could promenade, viewing the old formal gardens on one side and her new 'English' landscape on the other.

Wandering around this landscape is a journey of discovery where you unlock the pieces of her puzzle and gradually come to understand her dream-like vision. Most famous of all the ornamentation in the park is the Palladian Bridge, built entirely of marble in classic style. We love the expansive park with its Great Pond in the style of Capability Brown, which perfectly reflects each of the buildings around it. This huge lake was linked to smaller lakes by a system of channels and waterfalls.

Don't miss …

» … the Chinese village with 10 villas built in oriental style

» … a tour through Catherine Palace filled with treasures, in particular the Amber Room.

» … allowing a full day to see it all and walk around the Great Lake to fully appreciate the harmony of park and palace.

Best time to visit

Best in summer when the colourfully planted formal parterre reach their peak of flowering. In the summer, when there are regularly more than 7000 visitors a day, arrive early to avoid queuing.

Left: Neoclassic Cameron Gallery was a late addition with an impressive double staircase.
Above: 'Broderie' gardens complement the elaborate detail of the Palace façade.

Garden details

7, Sadovaya Str. Pushkin St. Petersburg Russia

25km S of St Petersburgh

Open daily 9am–8pm

The palace is open 10.30am to 5pm

Palace closed Tues and on the last Mon of every month

Tel +7 812 465 5308

+7 812 466 6674

www.pushkin-town.net

Chapter 4

SOUTHERN EUROPE

The quality of light in Southern Europe and the warm climate attracts people to settle permanently or at least to build summer houses and make gardens. Italy's gardens, especially those from Tuscany, have influenced garden design worldwide. Tuscan garden style, begun more than four centuries ago by the Tuscan aristocracy, shows man's desire to exert control over nature; these priniples remain important today.

In Andalusia, Spain, Moorish gardens have also influenced garden design with attention to decoration and the refreshing effects of running water. The Generalife in Granada is one of the oldest surviving Moorish gardens dating back to 1310; amazingly, it is as in vogue now as it was then.

View over Florence with pomegranate in flower.

Italy

I taly's best villa gardens date from the 15th, 16th and 17th centuries and were built by bishops, cardinals, counts, dukes and wealthy banking families. These individuals had a deep passion for their estates – and deep pockets! Gardens were a controlled form of nature, philosophically in line with the principles of the Church. In Italian gardens you'll notice an absence of flowers, with shades of green used to link the gardens into the landscape beyond. You'll notice the dominance of a main axis and cross axis design. This dissection of space, symmetry and proportion are really impressive. In the past, these gardens have been difficult to visit, being privately owned with eccentric opening hours. Gardens have been restored with loving care, respect, authenticity and funds from the Italian government. Visiting has never been easier.

Italy is the hottest country in Europe, yet its gardens keep cool. The Italian gardener is concerned with planting for shade: oaks, cypress, bay and box; pool, ponds and grottos and formal pools of water cool you down. Pots add focal points, particularly potted citrus. Hedges are trimmed into wonderful shapes. Simple symmetry is the key.

We plan our travels for early spring to escape the heat and beat the crowds. Gardens delight with rhododendrons, azaleas, camellias and spring bulb displays.

Classic example of Italian Renaissance garden design at Villa Gamberaia.

55. Isola Bella

Located on one of Borromean Islands in Lake Maggiore, this 17th-century garden and palatial villa is spectacular. We arrive via private boat from the lakeside town of Stresa and spend the day exploring the boat-shaped island, its 10 terraced gardens, many restaurants and the Borromeo family's baroque palace.

Timeline: 1630–1670

Description

There is something on this island for everyone. History buffs will be fascinated by the Borromeo family's vision; garden lovers will adore the plants and parterres; food lovers will love the simple northern Italian fare; and everyone appreciates the views of Lake Maggiore.

Enter the garden from the palace, having explored the subterranean vaults where cool grottoes of shell and black and white pebble-encrusted mosaics are decorated with marine motifs. Wander into the Courtyard of Diana to the theatrical terraces with flowering dogwoods, peacocks and parterres, all richly adorned with topiary, oversized statues and terracotta urns. Italians have a love affair with fountains and practical jokes and the two come together in 'water jokes', in which water is squirted onto unsuspecting visitors. These remain a feature of water gardens such as this one and Villa d'Este and Villa Lante.

From the top terrace you have the most pleasing view of the whole garden with French-inspired parterres to one side. You have a sense of being on a ship in the middle of the lake. You only to need close your eyes to conjure up another time, perhaps 1797 and the visit of Napoleon and Josephine with all its accompanying pomp and ceremony.

Don't miss …

» … the palace's interior.
» … The chance to ask your boat driver for a detour past other islands on your way to or back from Isola Bella.

Best time to visit

Spring: Azaleas, rhododendrons, dogwoods and bulbs

Summer: Lemons, oranges

Garden details

This garden can also be reached by boat from Arona, Stresa, Baveno, Pallanza and Laveno.
28050 Isola Bella
Lake Maggiore, Piedmont, Italy
Open daily 27 Mar–30 Sept, 9am–12pm, 1.30–5pm
Tel +39 0323 30556
Nearby is Isola Madre

Left: Gardens designed in a series of terraces with panoramic views over Lake Maggiore.
Above: The entire island has been remodelled into a dramatic sequence of terraces and resembles an ocean liner.

56. Villa Carlotta

Overlooking Lake Como, this jewel in the crown of Italy's north, is an 18th-century villa with original balustrade terrace, Italian parterres, views across to the Swiss alps and a relaxed English-style garden filled with thousands of tulips, azaleas and rhododendrons – all absolutely breathtaking in early spring.

Timeline: 1745

Description

On hot days it's pleasing to pass through the arbour of lemons, which offers a cool transition from one part of the garden to another. The patterns of light and shade and the play of shadows give a special dimension to the garden. Wisteria and sweet peas are the scents of spring, then star jasmine trained over walls and arches give this garden its overwhelming fragrant crescendo into summer. Teamed with lemons, orange blossom and gardenia, the perfume is exquisite.

This garden is the botanical collection of Carlotta (Duchess of Saxe-Meiningen) and includes ferns, palms, eucalypts, Japanese maples, roses, cork oaks, magnolias, camellia, banana, orchids and cacti. The moderate climate of this lakeside garden affords the surprising view of semi-tropical plants (banana and bamboo) backed by the snow-topped alps in the distance. Deep woods, fern gullies and secret gardens are all part of this magical journey.

Don't miss …

» … the marble sculpture exhibition inside the villa.

Best time to visit

A must for May when the thousands of tulips and 150 varieties of azaleas and rhododendrons flower in unison.

Garden details

Via Regina 2, 22019, Tremezzo, Lombardy
We suggest the journey via boat from Como
Open daily Mar–Oct, 10–11.30am, 2–4pm; Apr–Sept, 9am–6pm
Tel +39 0344 40405
www.villacarlotta.it

Left: Built on a steep slope overlooking Lake Como, the formal parterre and pond is a charming focal point.
Above: Patterns of light and shade give a special dimension to the garden.

57. Villa Chigi Cetinale

Garden lovers mustn't miss Villa Chigi Cetinale; also know as Lord Lambton's House or Villa, the garden of dedicated custodians, the late Lord Lambton and Mrs Ward. Villa Cetinale is a 16th-century villa in the Ancaiano district near Siena, Italy. Designed by the architect Carlo Fontana, the villa was built in the 1600s by Cardinal Flavio Chigi for Pope Alexander VII, Fabio Chigi. The gardens at Villa Cetinale are renowned as being amongst the most beautiful in Italy.

Timeline: Villa 1651, English garden 1978

'The Cetinale gardens are some of the finest in Italy – which is why one returns time and again'.   Meredith Chauncey, Tunbridge Wells, England

Description

We were thrilled to have Lord Lambton escort our group around the gardens just before his death in 2006. At the time, the gardens were filled with climbing roses, sweet peas, waterlilies, lilies and iris with grape-covered pergolas. In the spring, wisteria covers walls and the peony-filled borders are a sea of pink and purple. We strolled through fields of poppies and wild flowers with cypresses, olive trees and vineyards.

At the entrance of the villa lies the 'parterre de broderie' style courtyard, made famous in France, and which is a large component of Italian garden design. Made up of short box hedging, potted lemon trees and statues, it is best viewed from the first floor, where you can fully appreciate the intricate design.

Don't miss …

» … indulging yourself in the history of this place by staying a little longer in one of the two separate and self-contained villas located at Villa Cetinale, Casa Vin Santo or Cerbaia.

» … walking through the avenue of cypress that lead up the long grass avenue that climbs the hill and the monumental stairs (300 to be precise) to the distant hermitage on the hill's summit, (designed by architect Carlo Fontana, pupil of Gian Lorenzo Bernini).

» … two statues standing in front of the house 'Spring' and 'Summer' by Giuseppe Mazzuoli.

Best time to visit

Spring and summer: You will come back for more

Garden details

53018 Sovicille, Sienna, Tuscany, Italy
SS 73 Massa Maritima
14km SW of Siena
Signposts to Sovicille and Anciano

Open Mon–Fri, 9.30am–12.30pm by appointment only
Tel +39 0577 311 147
www.villacetinale.com/
info@villacetinale.com

Left: Soaring cypress, potted citrus and clipped topiary make up the classic elements of the Italian garden.
Above right: The 17th century château.
Below right: Lemon scent.

58. Villa Gamberaia

The journey to this garden is half the fun; travel by bus 45 minutes from Florence to Settignano and walk the rest of the way through olive groves and Tuscan villas, to this baroque masterpiece of Italian garden design.

Timeline: 1720

'If you get pure beauty, you get about the best thing God has to give".
Long ago, so spoke an old painter, and his words came back to me again
and yet again as on a June afternoon I strayed in Villa Gamberaia.'

C. Latham, *The Gardens of Italy*

Description

Enter through a charming sentinel of cypresses to experience the essence of Italian garden design. This garden has heart, soul and an intriguing history. From its stunningly simple quadrant pools and clipped topiary yew, to its exceptional position overlooking Florence and the Arno Valley, this garden is unparalleled.

Completed in the early 17th century by the Florentine noble Zanobi Lapi in the Tuscan style, the villa combines architectural features of both an urban palazzo and suburban villa. In the 18th century the property acquired its characteristic elements such as the cypress allée, bowling green, nymphaeum, grotto garden, boschi, parterre and lemon terrace. At the end of the 19th century, Princess Giovanna Ghika began the transformation of the parterre de broderie into the beautiful parterre d'eau. During the Second World War, German forces occupied the villa and the garden fell into disrepair. After the war the villa became the property of Marcello Marchi and then of his heirs Luigi Zalum and family, who have continued a high standard of restoration and conservation.

This garden is best appreciated from the first floor bedroom of the villa; so don't forget to ask if you can take a peep! From here you can see the baroque water garden is made up of four pools that reflect the Tuscan sky.

The garden is green with skyward-bound cypress, conical-shaped yew, grey-green oleander and colourful splashes of blue hydrangeas, citrus, pomegranates and bright potted geraniums. Terracotta pots are planted with lemons. Pots of pink geraniums along the balustrade provide colourful accents that match the warm colours of the Tuscan landscape.

Don't miss …

» … enjoy a coffee or gelato in Settignano before or after heading out.
» … the view from the southern end beneath a majestic cypress arcade.

» … a short stay in the guest-house is the perfect antidote to frenetic Firenze!
» … the grotto garden.

Best time to visit

A garden for all the senses … all year round.

Garden details

Via del Rossellino 72, 50135 Settignano-Florence, Tuscany
Open by appointment only
Tel (+39) 055 697 205
www.villagamberaia.com
Size 1.2 hectares
45 minutes out of Florence

Left: Potted geraniums and citrus decorate the summer garden.
Above: The view from the upstairs window is well worthwhile.

59. Villa d'Este

Some enterprising film producer should stage a new production of Shakespeare's *Midsummer Night's Dream* at Villa d'Este, for the garden is already full of magic and strange happenings. A series of terraces and intersecting paths demand the visitor explore. When the garden was first finished in the late 16th century using 'recycling' elements from nearby Hadrian's Villa, visitors were actors on the garden's stage, setting off the elaborate water fountains and tricks as they moved through it. This is one of the world's greatest water gardens.

Timeline: 1560–1575

Description

In 1605, Cardinal Alessandro d'Este gave the go-ahead to restore and repair the garden and the waterworks at the villa and also to create a new series of innovations to the layout of the garden and the decorations of the fountains. This water garden is terraced into the side of a hill that makes use of gravity to deliver water to every part of this garden – so bring your walking shoes! The good news is that although it's steep, it's deliciously cool as the water drops the temperature of the air by at least 15 degrees.

Magical fountains are in full swing: cascades, stone fountains, walls of water, a water organ, a terrace of 100 spouting stone faces—and not one water pump is used on site! All the fountains are operated by a 16th-century gravity-fed system. The movements of water are like symphonies of music with crescendo, diminuendo, forte, pianissimo and staccato – you won't want the music to stop.

Don't miss ...

» ... the fertility fountain.
» ... the organ fountain (1661) that plays every two hours from 10.30am.
» ... the walk of 100 fountains.

Best time to visit

Spring, summer

Garden details

Piazzo Trento, 1, 00019 Tivoli, Lazio

35km from Rome, Tivoli exit

Open all year except 1 Jan–1 May, Christmas Day. Open from 9am to one hour before sunset

Tel +39 0774 312 070

www.villadestetivoli.info

Left: The Fontana dell'Ovato (Oval Fountain), also called Fontana di Tivoli (Tivoli Fountain).
Above: The Fountain of Neptune.
Right: Take the walk down to the three large ponds.

60. Villa Lante

Bagnaia is a small and charmingly historical town in Northern Lazio, 45 minutes north of Rome, in the Province of Viterbo and within it is one of the most beautiful water gardens in the world. This garden's layout and design is so captivating that it alone enticed us to tour Europe. It's the best example of a garden of this style and era. We weren't disappointed, the water games, fascinating sculptures, water pools and rills have a sense of fun.

Timeline: 1573, restored 2004

Description

This is another magical Italian garden where water moves miraculously throughout the garden, taking you on a journey through a series of rooms, terraces, fountains, rills and shrimp-shaped ponds down the side of a hillside into the grand finale: a water parterre where, in Fountain of the Moors, four naked men hold up the arms of Cardinal Peretti Montalto!

Our favourite part is the third terrace, Fountain of the Table. It's a stone table with water running through it to cool large dishes of fruit and bottles of wine. We can imagine the cardinals and their friends sitting down to long lunches in the open air, enjoying this cool retreat. The water then falls into a shell-shaped basin and into a long crayfish or 'gambara'-shaped stone rill. The gambara is the symbol of Cardinal Gambara, a motif that is inscribed into friezes and facades through the garden.

The garden is perfectly symmetrical even down to a pair of small villas either side of the staircase. Tall plane trees provide essential shade and act as vertical elements that contrast with the flat lines of the water parterre.

Don't miss …

» … the Fountain of the Table.

» … Catena d'Acqua, the shrimp water feature.

» … the simple Italian fare available in the town of Bagnaia, a must for food lovers.

Best time to visit

Any day of the year

Garden details

Via Giacopo Barrozzi 71, 01031 Bagnaia (Viterbo), Lazio

5km E of Viterbo

Open all year, except public holidays; guided tours every half hour from 9am to one hour before sunset.

Tel +39 0761 288 088

Left: The Fountain of the Moors.
Above: The superbly restored water parterre.

61. Villa Orsini or Sacro Bosco, Sacred Wood

This garden, full of mythical stone creatures, is set in an ancient woodland with roots that break through the forest floor. It's like visiting another world at the top of the Faraway Tree. It will delight, scare, inspire and change your sense of perspective. This is one man's dream, so creative and magical – there is nothing like it in the world.

Timeline: 1552–1580

Description

The stone monsters (mythical creatures) date from 1542, the vision of Prince Vicino Orsini. Each one is positioned beautifully within deep green glades, surrounded by trees, moss and vines, and each reveals its message slowly, and only to the observant and reflective visitor. Vicino Orsini lost his wife then created this extraordinary garden to soothe his broken heart.

Pirro Ligorio, who also designed Villa d'Este and Villa Pia in the Vatican gardens, designed this garden for Orsini. He said an architect needs to do more than draw, paint and build – he needs to master astronomy, philosophy and the laws of perspective. Nowhere is this more true than here in the mystical centre of the Sacred Woods.

We love the giant sculptures, particularly Pegasus, symbol of the Farnese family, and the giant tortoise, reminding you to slow down on your journey. The wonderful elephant and leaning house will alter your perceptions – like topsy turvy.

After centuries of neglect it was rediscovered during the 1950s by surrealist artist Salvador Dali who found inspiration in the eclectic mix of the natural and the fantastical.

Don't miss …

» … taking an English speaking guide with you. They'll tell you all the stories that make up the allegories of the park.

» … any part of the park. Children will love the playful feel while adults will get in touch with their inner child!

Best time to visit

Any day of the year

Garden details

Parco dei Mostri, Bormarzo, Lazio

15km E of Viterbo

Open daily, 8.30am to sunset

Tel +39 0761 924 029

Nearby are Villa Lante and Villa Ruspoli

Size: 1.4 hectares

Left: Mythical creatures will fascinate all who visit.
Above: Pegasus and the giant tortoise.

62. Villa Vaticano, The Vatican Gardens

This garden of the Pope is a retreat, hidden from the world behind the high walls of the Vatican City. It's tricky to gain entry, you can't just wander through, you must be in a tour group with an application made at least a year in advance, in writing, and even then your visit may not eventuate! This is what you'd expect really, for this 'most secret' garden in the heart of Rome.

Timeline: 1505

Description

The Vatican Gardens date back to medieval times when vineyards and orchards extended to the north of the Apostolic Palace. In 1279, Pope Nicholas II enclosed this cultivated area with walls. Today these walls are no longer standing owing to a transformation at the beginning of the 16th century.

It's intriguing to walk where popes have walked for hundreds of years and to see a view of St Peter's unlike any other. Many gardens make up Vatican Gardens: follies, parterres, jasmine covered archways, commemorative trees, loggias, courtyards and fishponds. As you wander through you will notice an 'English landscape' feel, with expanses of well-tended lawn, spectacular trees, including pines and cedars and palms from all over the world.

At the finish of your tour, you will be delivered to a small unassuming door where you rejoin the tourist trail into the Sistine Chapel, a far cry from the peace and quiet of the Vatican gardens.

Don't miss …

» … the coral tree in full flower, which was a favourite of Pope John Paul II.

» … the jasmine arches.

» … the perfect garden pavilion, Villa Pia, designed by Pirro Ligorio in 1560 and built as a retreat for Pope Pius IV.

Best time to visit

June when the fragrant jasmine is flowering.

Garden details

Behind St Peter's Cathedral, Vatican City
Open all year, by appointment only. Book through the Vatican State Tourist office. Opening hours 9am–midday (last entrance). A 90-minute bus and walking tour of the Vatican Gardens is possible through the Vatican Office of Information for Pilgrims and Tourists located in Saint Peter's Square near the Vatican City Post Office. You can ask a guard for assistance in finding it. The tour of the gardens is offered every day at 10am, except Wednesdays and Sundays and originates at the office. Plan to arrive by 9.45am.
Tel +39 0669 884 466
Nearby are the Vatican museums, the Sistine Chapel and the City of Rome.

Left: St Peter's Dome.
Above: The arches full of scented jasmine.

Spain & Portugal

Portugal's mild climate has given rise to lush vegetation and beautiful gardens. As in Spain, Portuguese garden style has evolved from Roman, Moorish and Christian philosophies. Some gardens here date from the 9th century. Characteristic of the Portuguese style are the azulejos, the blue and white tiles that decorate loggias and huge water tanks. In Spain, the main influence, especially in Andalusia, is Mudejar (Muslim style). We love the ancient cultural roots of historic gardens in both countries. Our group tours are timed for early May to coincide with the Festival of the Patios in Cordoba. This festival sets the tone: colour, excitement, history, water, scent, fiesta and flamenco!

Fun, fiesta and flamenco: it's time to party! Bougainvilleas adorn walls like jewels.

63. Queluz

These romantic rococo gardens and pretty ornamented palace near Sintra are just two hours from Lisbon. Built for Portugal's King Pedro III in 1747, just before he was crowned, there is harmony between the palace and its gardens.

Description

This is a grand garden and it's not difficult picturing the royal family and court spilling out from the terrace of the palace into these gardens and being entertained by musicians and dancers.

Two intricate parterre gardens lie at the garden's heart: the Garden of Neptune, with two elaborate classic fountains; and the Garden of Malta, a sunken parterre, once a water tank. This second parterre is especially lovely surrounded as it is with beautiful curving steps that weave in and out 'like a dancing master's arabesque'. Alongside is the hanging garden, which is enclosed by classic balustrades, with lead statues and ceramic urns planted with soft pink geraniums to match the colour of the palace.

Below this set of formal gardens is a long canal covered in azulejos, typically Portuguese decorative tiles set in huge panels. Blue and white maritime scenes cover the interior of the canal with pastoral scenes on the exterior. This canal was filled with water for boat rides for special festive occasions for the royal family and the court.

Don't miss …

» … entering the garden through the palace where you will catch enticing glimpses of the garden from windows at the various levels.

» … the exquisite rococo detailing of the facade of the palace over the windows and doors that links so well with the ornamentation in the garden.

Best time to visit

Summer: The gardens are colourful with summer bedding and there are classical music concerts, part of the Sintra Music Festival

Garden details

Lg. do Palácio Nacional, 2745-191 Queluz, Lisbon, Portugal

Situated 15km from Old Quarter

Open daily except Tues, 10am–6pm

Tel +351 214 350 039

Left: Queluz Palace.
Above: Rococo details of the Garden of Malta, a sunken parterre with lollipop wisteria and topiary.

64. La Alhambra and El Generalife

This is the oldest garden in the world, built from 1302 and the best example of Moorish garden style. You'll find it near the town of Granada in the Sierra Nevada mountains in the south of Spain, which was under Arab rule until 1522 when it was conquered by King Ferdinand and Queen Isabella. The Alhambra and the adjacent palace, the Generalife, are perhaps the most charming series of gardens and courtyards we have ever seen. Once described by a Moorish poet as 'a pearl set in emeralds', they are the only European gardens to have maintained their original 14th-century lines.

Timeline: 1302

Description

This is a garden for the senses: for the sight of the honeycomb walls and detailed carving; for the sound of running water; for the smell of orange blossom, jasmine, magnolia and rose. The Alhambra palaces have highly ornate interiors with well-designed geometric exterior spaces. A skilful use of materials, textures and surfaces provides the most tactile effects.

The best examples are the Nasrid Palaces, with elaborate interior decoration and a spectacular interplay of light and shadow in the courtyards. But we also love Charles V Palace for its striking circular courtyard, impressive portico with columns and imposing facade. It was built later in Renaissance style after the Catholic monarchs took the city in 1492. You will find interesting exhibitions in this palace and the courtyard is the venue for concerts of the Granada Music and Dance Festival.

Rivulets and channels of water cool the courtyards, link rectangular, circular and square pools and draw you on through the complex. You follow the water to pass through light and dark spaces, inside and outside, flat and raised, matt and gloss, arid and moist, intricate and plain and to discover the Court of Lions, Court of Comares and Court of Myrtles, all framed with columns, arches, marble, basins, fountains and water jets.

The Patio of the Lions is one of most recognisable courtyards. Built in the 14th century, it is a charming example of a Persian pleasure garden. This open courtyard is divided into four parts by channels of water, which represent the Holy Rivers. Twelve carved marble lions support the central alabaster basin with four bun-shaped myrtles in each corner.

Don't miss …

» … the Generalife and don't be put off by the climb. Here you will find the most famous water garden, Court of the Long Pond.

» … a walking tour with an official guide, who will explain the fascinating history. And get there early before the crush of visitors.

Best time to visit

May: Fragrant spring blossom

Late June–early July: Music and Dance Festival held over 17 days at the Generalife

Garden details

Palacio de Carlos V, Granada

Open Nov–Feb, Mon–Sun, 8.30am–6 pm; Fri–Sat, 8pm–9:30 pm; Mar–Oct, Mon–Sun, 8.30am–8pm, Tues–Sat, 10pm–11.30pm

Tel +34 902 44 12 21 or +34 958 22 09 12

www.alhambra.org

Left: Patio de la Acequia, El Generalife.
Above right: Stone lions in the Court of Lions support the central basin.
Below right: Intimate courtyards can only be seen from the windows of the Alhambra Palace.

65. Alcazar de los Reyes Cristianos, Castle of the Christian Kings

Built in 1328 and expanded by the Moors, this historic palace-fortress in the heart of Cordoba is a large compound of massive walls and towers with extensive gardens, pools and fountains. Most of the gardens here have been recently remodelled and are often referred to as Spain's finest.

Timeline: 1328

Description

Visitors have an elevated view of the garden as they step out from the fortress. The grand scale and formal design laid out below is impressive. It's a 19th-century re-creation of the original 15th-century gardens with fountains, ponds and hedges arranged on a series of levels. A long pool stretches along the main axis of the garden with water jets interspersed along the entire length. The pool is edged with colourful flower gardens and sweet-smelling citrus trees. An impressive avenue of clipped conifer columns echoes the architecture of the fortress.

The focal point of this vista is a statue of Christopher Columbus kneeling before King Ferdinand and Queen Isabella. It's a wonderful symbol as he pitched his journey to the monarchs here just before his historic journey to the Americas.

The formal garden features circular and rectangular beds edged with clipped box and filled with roses and other sweet-smelling shrubs. The sweet scents and running water of the garden is a reminder of its Moorish past.

Don't miss …

» … the Courtyard of Oranges at the entry to the Alcazar, an ancient grove of oranges that is easy to miss.

» … the charming interior patios within the Alcazar with central fountain and pool and planted with loquats, citrus, myrtle and jasmine.

Best time to visit

Spring: Planting of brightly coloured geraniums

High summer: Dahlia time is also very colourful but the weather can be very warm

Garden details

Caballerizas Reales, Córdoba, Andalucia, 14004

Located next to the Guadalquivir River and near the Mezquita in Cordoba

Open May–Jun, 10am–2pm, 5.30–6.30pm; Jul–Aug, 8.30am–2.30pm; Sept–14 Oct, 10am–2pm, 5.30–6.30pm; 15 Oct–30 Apr, 10am–2pm, 4.30–6.30pm; closed Mon

Tel +351 957 420 151

Left: A recreated 15th century masterpiece.
Above: View over the garden back to the fortress.

Chapter 5

THE AMERICAS

The Americas stretch from Alaska in the north to Terra del Fuego in the south with the full range of climatic zones in between: desert, mountain ranges, open prairie, subtropical and cold temperate. Gardens embrace all types of plants from these regions, from tough, hardy, desert-loving survivors to the tropical delights of Central America. There is inspiration for all here.

Ivory, elegant and fragrant, the Bull Bay Magnolia (M. grandiflora) has its home in the USA.

Canada

Canadian gardens have a brief but powerful season because of their short summers. A legacy of garden making exists and public gardens such as Butchart and Casa Loma Minter have resulted from individual endeavours. Private gardens have been influenced in the main by those of the United Kingdom, although French Canadian gardens in the east have a certain French style and formality that links them to their cultural roots.

Fiery canopy of Butchart Gardens in the fall.

66. Butchart Gardens

It's a 90-minute relaxing ferry ride from Vancouver city to Vancouver Island. A short drive from there is Butchart, which has 22 gardens in an ever-changing succession of flower. It was Jennie Butchart who saw the potential for garden beauty in the disused quarry close by the house she shared with her husband, cement baron Robert Butchart. Her reclaimed quarry gardens became known as Butchart and are now visited by more than a million visitors a year.

Timeline: 1904

Description

Thousands of tulips, hyacinths and daffodils morph into spectacular bedding displays followed by roses and dahlias, and baskets dripping with tuberous begonias and fuchsias. These original flower basket designs are copied the world over.

We've been visiting Butchart for 30 years and it gets better every year. This is a real display garden, the world's first. The standard of horticulture is impeccable from the front gate where flower baskets fill the Shade House, past flower-filled borders to the Rose Garden, at its peak in early summer. Turn up the steps to the terrace overlooking the Sunken Garden (which was the old quarry) and the panorama unfolds before you. A path winds through flower-filled beds, punctuated with magnificent trees; guaranteed to take your breath away and to be captured on camera.

Speak to the gardeners as you walk through. What more can you ask of a garden still in the hands of the family who created it?

Don't miss …

» … lunch in the Butchart family home, a splendid experience with a view of the garden (make a prior booking).
» … the Ross fountain display at the bottom of the old quarry with its changing water fountain display.

Best time to visit

Late March–mid June: Spring flowers excel

Mid June–September: Summer shrubs bloom

July: Fireworks at night

October–November: Autumn colour, especially in the Japanese Garden

December–January: Christmas lights, displays and skating exhibition

January–late March: Winter snowdrops, witch hazel and berry bushes

Garden details

800 Benvenuto Avenue, Brentwood Bay, Vancouver Island, British Columbia, V8M 1J8

1 hour, 35 minute ferry trip from Vancouver city, then 30 minutes car drive from the ferry terminal to Butchart Gardens

Open daily at 9am (Christmas Day open at 1pm

Tel +1 250 652 4422

www.butchartgardens.com

Size 22 hectares

Left: Sunken garden, once a quarry, is testament to the vision of Jenny Butchart.
Above right: The suburb standard of horticulture attracts millions of garden lovers each year.
Below right: The Japanese Garden.

67. The Toronto Music Garden

This garden is a living interpretation of Bach's musical genius. This romantic concept is set on the shores of Lake Ontario, in downtown Toronto and is a collaboration between landscape architect, Julie Moir Messervy and cellist, Yo-Yo Ma. It is based on the musical structure of Bach's Suite No. 1 for solo cello. Paths wind, twist and spiral in an intriguing musical way, with a planting scheme to match.

Timeline: 1999

Description

The garden is divided into sections, in line with the movements of the music. You move with the music through the garden, starting with the Prelude, which is an undulating river scene with the feeling of a free-flowing river. The Allemande is next, an ancient German dance, represented here in a birch grove featuring wandering trails that swirl into intimate sitting areas.

Next you reach the exuberant Courante, an Italian/French dance, represented as a swirling pathway through a wildflower meadow. It makes you want to lift your skirts and swirl to the music. At the top a maypole spins in the wind.

Now the contemplative Sarabande, an ancient Spanish dance form with an inward arching circle enclosed by evergreens. On to the Minuet, a formal flower parterre that reflects Bach's period. The finale is the Gigue, giant grass steps that dance you down to the outside world.

Under the guardianship of Toronto City Parks, the garden is renewed each year with an inspiring palette of perennial plants, mainly soft ornamental grasses that ensure a freshness and vigour. Most of the plants are used en masse to create volume and harmony like a symphony.

Don't miss …

» … interlocking sweeps of deciduous grasses with highlights of flowering plants, such as the toffee apple shapes of allium.

» … the huge boulders that add solidity to this otherwise ephemeral scheme.

Left: Swaying grasses make you want to dance through this garden.
Above: Maypole centrepiece in the wildflower meadow of the 'Courante' section.

Best time to visit

Summer: Grasses and perennials are fully grown and flowering

Garden details

475 Queens Quay West, Toronto, Ontario, L9Y 4T9
Open all year round, no admission fee
Tel +1 416 973 4000
www.toronto.ca/parks/music_index.htm
Size 1.3 hectares

68. Casa Loma

Set in the suburbs of Toronto lies an architectural fantasy called Casa Loma. Don't let the gaudy architecture put you off; this is one of Canada's garden gems.

Description

What started out in 1911 as the European dream of Toronto financier Sir Henry Pellatt ended up as an enormous castle, complete with ballroom, battlements and secret passageways. The castle is surrounded by an extensive English-style 'Gentlemen's Garden', today filled with roses, rhododendrons, perennials, bulbs and many rare Canadian wildflowers. The seasonal bedding plant displays are beautifully designed and well maintained.

We like the Lower Terrace in June when the delphiniums, iris, campanula and late tulips bloom among the fountains and formal annual flowerbeds. The pure white of the trunks of the birch trees growing in this area is indicative of the Canadian landscape.

Don't miss …

» … 75 different varieties of roses in flower, including their own Casa Loma Rose, in the Rose Garden. There are old-fashioned David Austin English roses and floribunda roses in the garden and climbers on the rose arbour leading through into the Secret Garden filled with peonies.

» … a self-guided tour for a glimpse inside the castle.

Best time to visit

May: Rare spring trillium and other shade loving perennials like primrose, fritillaria, anemone, bergenia and rhododendron fill the shady gardens under the trees

June: Roses

July: Astilbes, rare hostas, calla lilies, daylilies, phlox and yarrow look sensational

October: Maples colour and the autumn grasses and chrysanthemum show is worth seeing

Garden details

1 Austin Terrace, Toronto, ON M5R 1X8

Open daily to view the house, 9.30am–5.00pm; gardens open May–Oct, 9.30am–4.00pm

Free access to gardens only 12 May, 9 Jun, 14 Jul, 11 Aug, 8 Sept, 6 Oct

Tel +1 416 923 1171

www.casaloma.org

Left: Eclectic architecture is softened with a series of garden rooms.
Above right: Terrace gardens feature autumn Chrysanthemums.
Below right: Potted plant collections decorate the café terrace.

United States of America

The 'Grand Tour' of Europe influenced Americans, particularly those on the East Coast, in the same way it did the English during the late 19th century. For the Americans, the strongest influence on garden design came from England, first with the English landscape style, and later by the introduction at the turn of the 20th century of the 'Arts and Crafts' style.

In the rolling hills where Pennsylvania meets Delaware, you find the Brandywine Valley, a place of such serene rural beauty that it's hard to remember that this is the sight of some of the bloodiest battles of the American revolution (1777). Philadelphia is only 50 kilometres away so noisy freeways are just a good stone's throw over lines of beautiful trees. Lovely stone houses sit in this gentle landscape; rolling hills, fields of dried corn stalks, faded yellow sunflowers, split rail fences, horse pastures and narrow country roads. You can chase the fall colours all through this beautiful valley! Along the way you will discover two of America's finest gardens, the two horticultural masterpieces of Longwood and Chanticleer.

Longwood Gardens, the dream of Pierre du Pont, one of America's finest gardens.

69. Longwood

Waltz through the lofty conservatories, dramatic water fountain displays and immaculate grounds of one of the world's great gardens, and you'll leave impressed by the passion and imagination of its creator. Pierre DuPont's Longwood Gardens in Pennsylvania is one of the greatest gardens of the world.

Timeline: Arboretum 1798, garden 1906

Description

Picture a staggering 445 hectares of gardens, woodlands and meadows; 20 outdoor gardens; 20 indoor gardens within 1.6 hectares of heated greenhouses and 11,000 different species of plants! In 1906, Pierre Du Pont, a wealthy industrialist, purchased the property in order to save an historic collection of trees from the lumber mill.

Make your way down past the open-air theatre into the Flower Garden Walk, just a short distance from the house. The flower borders are an eye-catching mix of annuals and perennials, carefully graduated in colour from cool purples to warm reds finishing with creams and whites.

Then head to Pierce's Wood for change of scene. Magnificent sugar maples are under-planted with flowers of lace-cap and oak-leaf hydrangeas. A large lake stretches ahead reflecting a soft autumnal scene, its classic rotunda making an elegant focus. Walk around this lake and drink in its serenity, such a dramatic contrast to the structured design of the flower gardens.

The Water Garden was restored in 1992 with 6 large and 12 small ponds, 600 jets and a water staircase, a theatrical experience with music and choreographed displays.

Don't miss …

» … the display of giant Amazon waterlilies (*Victoria amazonica*), the largest of all the waterlilies. The plant's leaves reach three metres in diameter! In this protected courtyard, five pools grow an extensive range of aquatic plants.

» … the Conservatory Terrace at 2pm to witness the spectacle of the fountains. Inspired by Chicago's 1893 World's Columbian Exposition, Pierre Du Pont set out to create the ultimate fountain display at Longwood. A system of pumps propels 45,500 litres of water a minute high up into the sky—a dramatic spray that shoots 40 metres from the ground. This Main Fountain terrace garden is eclectic and ornate—and we all agree this is water theatre at its best. Just as Pierre Du Pont would have expected it to be.

Best time to visit

The garden has something to offer every day of the year. The main fountain operates from 9am – 5.45pm daily 15 April–15 Oct

Garden details

1001 Longwood Rd, Kennett Square, Pennsylvania, 19348

Open every day

Take the US Route 1 an easy drive from Philadelphia or Wilmington

Tel +1 610 383 1000

www.longwoodgardens.org

Size 445 hectares

Left: The woodland takes centre stage when leaves change colours for fall.
Above right: Everchanging flower displays in the conservatory, here the Chrysanthemums are featured.
Below right: The Water Garden now restored is a theatrical experience with musical displays.
Next page right: Classic elements decorate the Long Walk.
Next page left: Lakeside gazebo.

70. Huntington Botanic Gardens

Originally the private estate of Henry Huntington, who bought this 48-hectare parcel of land in San Marino, just outside Los Angeles. He developed a series of serious plant collections into botanical gardens with desert, herb, rose, Shakespeare, camellia, Japanese, Australian, palm, jungle, subtropical and Chinese gardens.

Timeline: 1903

Description

Henry Huntington developed the gardens with the assistance of horticulturist William Hertrich, who stayed another 20 yeas after Henry's death in 1927. The garden captures the depth of Henry's passion for California; there is a sense that nothing is impossible, all you need is the vision (and money) to conceive it.

Among the most remarkable areas is the Desert Garden for which the garden is famous. It shows the passion of William Hertrich and displays 2500 species of cacti and succulents from dry land regions. As it has matured, parts of this garden have become gargantuan. There are euphorbia and aloes the size of huge trees!

The Australian Garden, originally a planting of 1000 eucalypts (1943), was a fire hazard so many trees were removed and interplanted with an extensive range of Australian flora.

The Japanese Garden is the most tranquil with its Moon Bridge, traditional Japanese house and Zen garden. Henry employed a Japanese family to dress in traditional clothes and stroll through the garden to give it ambiance and authenticity! The camellia collection here is one of the largest in the country.

Don't miss …

» … the Art Gallery, home to Gainsborough's 'The Blue Boy' and Lawrence's 'Pinkie'.

» … the Chinese garden, the largest outside China.

Best time to visit

April: Walk through a tunnel of wisteria

May–June: Roses

October: Orchids and herbs

July–August: Chamber Music Summer Festival

Garden details

1151 Oxford Rd, San Marino, California, 91108

Open Mon, Wed, Thurs, Fri, midday–4.30pm; Sat–Sun, 10.30am–4.30pm

Tel +1 626 405 2100

www.huntington.org

Size 48 hectares

Left: Moon bridge into the Japanese Garden.
Above: Desert Garden with an extraordinary collection of succulents and cacti.

71. Chanticleer

Chanticleer came into being when a large parcel of land close to the Main Line of the Pennsylvania Railroad was purchased by Adolph Rosengarten Sr. Adolph, like other wealthy merchants from Philadelphia was keen to escape the city heat and built Chanticleer as a summerhouse in 1913.

Timeline: 1913–1990

Description

Originally the estate was a beautiful park-like landscape, although extensions in 1924 converted this to a year-round residence with pool terrace. Most of the current pleasure garden has been developed since 1990. Originally, the estate was known for its majestic trees and verdant lawns. Today, the trees and lawns remain, planted with white daffodils. The focus now is on plant combinations with emphasis on foliage rather than flowers.

A series of intimate courtyards surround the house. The entrance courtyard is tropical with an Italianate fountain and subtropical exotic plants: pineapple lilies, taro, gingers and passion flowers. These courtyards are the framework for unusual combinations of hardy and tropical plants.

On the Chanticleer Terrace are spring-flowering cherries underplanted with hydrangeas. Walk down to the large pond constructed as a mirror for the trees that surround it. Dense planting around this and three smaller ponds constitutes a significant garden. When Minder House, the home of Adolph, was razed in 1999 a new ruin was built over the foundations. Carved marble and other stone define the spaces in what is now the Ruin Garden. A dry Gravel Garden alongside the ruin is planted with lavenders and ornamental grasses and has enchanting views to the ponds. A vegetable garden is contained inside a fence of espaliered apples and pears. There is a mix of vegetables grown for taste and ornament. This garden complements a cut-flower garden. A serpentine of cedars, boulders and agronomic crops undulates through a mown hillside.

A woodland garden carpeted with Asian groundcovers and full of rarities leads to a water garden surrounded by exuberant perennials. Sculptural, homemade seats, benches, wrought-iron fences and bridges highlight the uniqueness and personal nature of the garden.

Don't miss ...

» ... the courtyard gardens close to the house.
» ... the Adirondack chairs painted pink to match the autumn flowering crocus.

Best time to visit

Spring: Daffodils in lawn, tulips, bluebells, dogwoods
Autumn: Crocus, autumn colour

Garden details

786 Church Rd, Wayne, Pennsylvania, 19087
Open Apr–Oct, Wed–Sun, 10am–.5pm; May–Aug, 10am–8pm.
Tel +1 610 687 4163
www.chanticleergarden.org
Size 12 hectares

Left: A series of intimate courtyards.
Above right: Giant sun-loving bromeliads, Alcantarea imperialis.
Below right: Adirondack chairs well placed for the view.

72. Lotusland

The name says it all – this is a dreamy place. Exotic and strange, this vision of opera star Ganna Walska, who turned away from the world outside to focus on her spiritual life within these walls. It's a unique 15-hectare estate and botanic garden situated in the foothills of Montecito to the east of the city of Santa Barbara. Madame Ganna Walska, who owned the property from 1941 until her death in 1984, created the gardens now covering the estate.

Timeline: 1941–1984

Description

Madame Walska created elaborate gardens around her California home and eventually became a recluse here. We love her abalone-edged swimming pool, with coral islands and giant clamshell fountains and is surrounded by more than 100 giant South African aloes.

There are no less than 17 different parts of this garden to see; the blue garden with blue Atlas cedars and Chilean wine palms growing out of a sea of blue fescue grass and blue chalksticks; the brooding fern garden with Australian tree ferns and staghorns; and the bromeliad garden, situated under ancient oaks.

It is a privilege to enter Walska's world and experience her weird gigantic collection of botanic oddities. Before her death, Madame Walska established the non-profit Ganna Walska Lotusland Foundation, which now preserves this unrivalled botanical treasure.

Don't miss …

» … the back of the Blue Garden where you will find Queensland kauri (*Agathis robusta*), bunya-bunya (*Araucaria bidwillii*) and hoop pine (*Araucaria cunninghamii*), all conifers from Australia. There are also two camphor trees (*Cinnamomum camphora*), native to China and Japan.

» … the new topiaries created in shapes reflecting Madame Walska's original topiary circus. Children will love this. The new 'zoo' of 26 animals includes a camel, gorilla, giraffe and seal as well as other frames shaped as chess pieces and geometric shapes.

Best time to visit

April: Giant aloe in full flower

Garden details

695 Ashley Rd, Santa Barbara, California, 93108
Open mid-Feb–mid Nov, 10am, 1.30pm tours with advance reservations required because this is a public garden operating in a private neighbourhood.
Tel +1 805 969 9990
www.lotusland.org
Size 15 hectares

Left: Cascading and golden barrel cacti create a dramatic entrance.
Above: The weird world of Ganna Walska.

73. Valentine

This is the modern hallmark garden of landscape architect Isabelle Green, who was inspired by of aerial views of farm fields. The garden, built in 1980, for Mrs Carol Valentine appears to have been magically flattened into a two-dimensional carpet.

Timeline: 1980

Description

You enter the garden through a simple dry courtyard with slate paving patterns, gravel, water and Australian weeping eucalypts enclosed within white walls. These white walls make up the boundaries of the garden and give the garden its modern feel.

Using the opportunity of the sloping site and the home's position within it, Greene has created flat planes planted like an abstract painting. The garden, designed to be viewed from high balconies, features rivers of rocks; a 'lava flow' of senecio interrupted by spiny agave; a knobbly, rust-coloured rug of sedum; vibrant-coloured gardens; cool grey granite chips, gravel and terraces. This is pattern making at its best.

This garden is never watered, and because of the dry land plant palette it uses, it has becomes a great lesson for those gardening in dry climates.

Don't miss …

» … the espaliered fig on the wall.
» … the views from the house (if you can manage it).

Best time to visit

Lovely all year round

Garden details

Montecito, Santa Barbara, California, USA
Open by appointment only

Left: Masterful use of drought tolerant plants.
Above: A series of terraces best viewed from the upper balcony, with gardens planted like an abstract painting.

74. Mount Vernon

This estate of Martha and George Washington, the first President of the United States of America, was restored in 1936 from diaries he kept between 1748 and 1799. Located on the banks of the Potomac River in Washington, the gardens are bounded by a 'ha-ha' sunken fence on three sides and the river on the fourth. The garden is laid out in five separate areas: botanic garden; upper garden, which evolved into a pleasure garden; a lower kitchen garden; a vineyard of mostly fruit trees and experimental plantings of grasses, grains and vegetables; and a landscape garden with lawns typical of 18th-century design. These gardens give a glimpse into Washington's hopes for his new nation.

Timeline: 1748–1799, restored 1936

'I am once more seated under my own Vine and Fig-tree, and hope to spend the remainder of my days … in peaceful retirement, making political pursuits yield to the more rational amusement of cultivating the earth.'

George Washington to Dr James Anderson 7 April 1797 from Washington's Gardens at Mount Vernon by Mac Griswold

Description

George Washington's gardens were a cornucopia of plenty for the kitchen; a medicine chest; and a laboratory for economic botany. Washington was a model farmer and Mount Vernon evolved as a working farm. In fact, there were five working farms, each a complete unit with its own workforce of slaves, livestock and equipment. Washington planted 60 different crops. He developed elaborate rotation systems to rest the soil. Even while George Washington was on the battlefield he sent letters for the upkeep of the farm and garden. When he died in 1799, the property had expanded to more than 3000 hectares.

The house is quite modest for a United States president and offers an insight into the family and the history of the estate. We were surprised to see such simplicity and purity. Flower and kitchen gardens run parallel to the facade of the house and the orangery makes a return wing at one end. Peaches, pears, apples and cherries are espaliered on the walls.

The Pleasure Garden in the Upper Gardens features the bulbs, annuals and perennials that were grown by George Washington. Note the fruiting fig and the flowering cherry and the box parterre in the shape of the fleur-de-lys. The Kitchen Garden on the Lower Parterre is planted with historically correct varieties of fruits and vegetables. Today the educational components for children are extensive with adventure maps, scouting trails, animals to meet and a new Orientation Centre.

Don't miss ...

» ... the enclosed Botanic Garden, behind the Upper Garden, where Washington experimented with pecan and other nuts, root crops for animal fodder. Be sure to find his 'little garden'.

» ... look for the key to the Bastille in Paris given to the Washingtons by the French Revolution's La Fayette.

Best time to visit

October: Harvest time when fruit and vegetable are maturing

Spring: Lovely when dogwoods, cherries and cercis come to flower

Garden details

3200 Mount Vernon Memorial Highway, Mount Vernon, Virginia 22121

Located 25 km S of Washington DC

Open every day of the year (incl. holidays and Christmas), Apr–Aug, 8am–5pm; Mar, Sep, Oct, 9am–5pm; Nov–Feb, 9am–4pm

Tel +1 703 780 2000

Left: Flower and kitchen garden of George Washington.
Above right: Pleasure Garden.
Below right: Parrot tulips.

75. Dumbarton Oaks

This garden of Robert and Mildred Bliss was designed by leading landscape architect Beatrix Farrand, and remains one of the great 20th-century gardens. Inspired by contemporary English designers such as Jekyll and Lutyens, this garden shows a love of French and Italian Renaissance. Farrand's great achievement was to combine these influences with a palette of native American plants, giving the garden a strong connection to the surrounding landscape.

Timeline: 1921–1947

Description

Three principles govern the plan at Dumbarton Oaks. Progressive informality in the design; materials and plantings as the gardens recede down the slopes to the north and east (plants were chosen for their beauty in winter as well as in spring and autumn); and it was agreed the garden needed spaces for living. Enclosed areas, 'garden rooms', were created for family use and entertaining, including a swimming pool, tennis court (later replaced with a pebble garden), and open air theatre.

The gardens at Dumbarton Oaks have a romantic, old-world atmosphere, due in part to the European trees that frame the views and also to the understated use of ornament.

A *Magnolia grandiflora* is espaliered against the house, making a grand European use of an American tree. The garden is linked to the house by an orangery, which overlooks the terraced gardens. Because of the steep site, carefully designed steps and a series of narrow terraces were installed, made to fit the natural levels. No flight is more than six steps. A magnificent pair of star magnolias (*Magnolia stellata*) flank the box terrace. The Fountain Terrace contains two ponds with cherub fountains covered in moss. The gardens were donated to Harvard University and are open to the public.

Don't miss …

» … the huge interlaced root system of the English beech, between Lovers' Lane Pool and the Fountain Terrace. Take note of the finials and sculpture carved from Indiana limestone and mostly designed by Beatrix Farrand.

» … a visit to the museum next door.

Best time to visit

Mid March through April: Spring bulbs, cherry trees, forsythia, wisteria, azaleas, dogwood, lilacs, akebia and star magnolia

May: Lilacs, perennial borders, clematis, roses, peonies and fringe tree

June: Perennial borders, clematis, roses, Magnolia grandiflora and canna

July–August: Perennial borders, day lilies, fuchsia, gardenias, agapanthus and oleanders

Late September–October: Chrysanthemums

Garden details

1703 32nd St, Northwest, Washington, D.C. 20007
The entrance to the gardens is at R and 31st streets, two blocks East of Wisconsin Avenue in Georgetown.
Open daily (except Mon), 15 Mar–31 Oct, 2–6pm; 1 Nov–14 Mar, 2–5 pm; closed during inclement weather, federal holidays and Christmas Eve
Tel +1 202 339 6401
www.doaks.org
DumbartonOaks2008@doaks.org

Left: Classic pool in this simple terrace.
Above: Autumn colour in golden shades of Chrysanthemums.

Chapter 6

AFRICA

Desert landscapes, such as the Sahara, make up most of the continent with forest only accounting for one tenth of the total land area. The climate is mostly tropical or subtropical although there are temperate areas in the north and south. In these areas garden history has been greatly influenced by English garden style. The European influence, and in particular the English garden with lush lawns, by the English colonial occupation, exotic plants such as zinnias and jacaranda, canna lily, frangipani, bougainvillea and hibiscus, were favourites in the mid-nineteenth century and this tradition continues today. Seeds were originally brought in from Britain.

In recent time an interest has developed to recognise and protect indigenous flora. Many of our garden plants have their origins in Africa including agapanthus, gazania, protea and babiana. The fynbos of South Africa is just a part of its incredible rich and diverse flora. More species occur naturally here every square metre that anywhere else on earth!

The King Protea, Protea cynaroides, grows wild in the mountains of the Western Cape, including Table Mountain. Also pictured are the orange flowers of the common pincushion, Leucospermum cordifolium, and Castle Rock, the mountain peak directly behind the Garden at Kirstenbosch.

Morocco

The Kingdom of Morocco nestles on the north-west tip of Africa and is separated from the rest of Africa by the towering Atlas Mountains and the Sahara Desert. The climate is Mediterranean with cool breezes on the Mediterranean and Atlantic coasts, becoming warmer inland and hot in the interior. Winters are wet in the north, typical of Mediterranean climate, and dry and cold in the south.

A typical urban house (*riad*) is inward-looking, with a central decorated courtyard. Ambience is important with the sound of rippling water from a central fountain and the fragrance of citrus blossom. An arched colonnade offers shade and access to living areas with bedrooms upstairs. The walls and archways wrap the house in cool temperatures and the water features enliven the scene.

The ceramic floor tiles of a courtyard within the Bahia Palace, Morrocco.

76. Les Jardin de la Mamounia

This legendary hotel opened in 1923 and has always been a popular rendezvous for celebrities. A bar suite is named in honour of Sir Winston Churchill, who visited every winter for 20 years to paint in Marrakesh in winter, the olive trees and the snow-capped Atlas mountain peaks. La Mamounia's name derives from the legendary gardens, known three centuries ago as "Arset el Mamoun," named for Prince Moulay Mamoun, son of Sultan Sidi Mohamed Ben Abdellah, ruler of Marrakech in the 18th century.

Timeline: 1923

Description

Step back in time to the legendary Moroccan Palace, La Mamounia, is now a hotel, decorated in Moorish and art-deco styles. Located within the famous 12th century ramparts of Marrakesh and surrounded by idyllic parklike gardens, La Mamounia Hotel is just a short walk from the maze of busy souks and the city's historic landmarks.

This palace is the essence of the Moroccan Art de Vivre, composed of elements such as stylish tiles, carved stone, water rills, internal courtyards and ponds to convey a relaxed feel. The courtyard gardens are secreted away from the bustle of the street and offer peaceful cool retreats full of subtropical plants. Nothing is more romantic than the silhouette of the palm trees, balmy air, opulent furnishings and an outlook from your room to indigo in blue twilight with the skyline of Marrakech in lights.

Don't miss …

» … the inner courtyards.

Best time to visit

The garden and park can be visited any day but the hotel won't be open until spring 2009 after extensive renovations.

Garden details

La Mamounia Hotel

Avenue Bab Jdid Marrakech

15 minutes from airport, 5 minutes from railway station

Open daily

Tel +212 (0)24 388 600

Size: 7 hectares

Left: The grand entrance of the most famous hotel in Morocco.
Above: The simple and serene interior courtyard.

77. Le Jardin Majorelle

This garden was conceived by French painter Jacques Majorelle in 1924 after he settled in Marrakesh, keen to capture its charm on canvas. He bought this property on the edge of a palm grove and built a home in the likeness of a Moroccan palace with simple architecture, water ponds and fountains. Then he set about planting the garden.

Timeline: 1924

Description

Jacques Majorelle scoured the world for plants: cactus, yucca, waterlilies, jasmine, bougainvillea and set about making a tropical paradise. The garden, his source of inspiration and relaxation, became so famous he opened it to the public. A severe car accident cut short his time in Marrakesh and he returned to France. The garden remained open but deteriorated until it was bought by Yves Saint Laurent, who undertook extensive restoration.

We love the colour of the house, now a museum of Islamic art, which is painted a powerful blue called Majorelle Blue. There are touches of this blue through the garden, edging the pool and in fountains and windows. Large pots of flowering plants are a signature of Majorelle, the blue combining dramatically with lemon and clear green.

Palm trees have been collected from all over the world and lend the exotic ambience of a tranquil oasis. As you walk through a forest of tall bamboo, you get the feeling of a lush, leafy jungle.

Don't miss …

» … the traditional Moroccan aesthetic, the decorative touches make this garden special. The garden is not huge so you can see it all.

Best time to visit

Early morning is best while the fragrance lingers and before it gets too hot.

Garden details

Jardin Marjorelle, Maroc

Open   Oct–May, 8am–5pm; Jun–Sept, 8am–6pm

Tel +212 (0)24 301 852

www.jardinmarjorelle.com

Left: A cool square of water.
Above: An exciting mix of cactus is set off by the Majorelle blue villa.

South Africa

The plants and landscapes of South Africa are unique and mind-blowingly colourful. Australia and South Africa were aligned about 200 million years ago when South America, Africa, Madagascar, Antarctica, India, other parts of South Asia and Australia were included in a greater continent–Gondwana. The fossil records from this time are the same – suggesting the plants of these continents evolved at the same time. South Africa's flora is now some of the most beautiful and unusual in the world.

Under the aegis of the Dutch East and West India companies, gardens were laid out under principles of the Dutch classical garden. Gardening in South Africa began in 1652 when Jan van Riebeeck, the first Commander of the Cape, arrived to establish a refreshment station for the ships of the Dutch East India Company. He planted a vegetable garden on the north slope of Table Mountain very close to the present location of Kirstenbosch Botanic Garden.

In 1913, a new concept of gardening came to the forefront of South African horticulture and that was the development of indigenous-only botanic gardens. The first of these was Kirstenbosch, and others followed in all the other climatic zones. Here you find the essence of South African plants, planted in gardens that echo the real landscape of the country.

Our travels have taken us to South Africa in spring to see the wildflowers. Time your visit to journey through paddocks of African daisies, pincushion bush, protea and pig's face.

Vygies, pronounced fay-gh-ease, also known as ice-plants or midday flowers, are small shrubby succulents that make colourful carpets.

78. Durban Botanic Garden

These are the oldest gardens in South Africa and their history is tumultuous: they survived two world wars and the era of apartheid. They were established in 1849 on the eastern slopes of the Berea Ridge as an experimental site for the growing of tropical crops for the colony. The advent of a new age has seen the rebirth of botanic gardens around the world and the reinvention of this one. It is now one of Durban's top tourist attractions, drawing visitors to its collections of indigenous cycads (including the unique Wood's cycad), palms and bromeliads.

Timeline 1849

Description

In 1948, Durban—or Port Natal as it was then—was little more than two dirt streets with shabby wood-and-iron buildings. Yet some enterprising locals met and agreed to pursue the development of a botanic garden in Durban. The scheme was to assist the introduction to the region of plants of possible economic value. The gardens might also supply Kew botanists with plants new to science.

A Scot called Mark McKen, a first-rate plants man and plant collector, who had hands-on experience working in the old Bath Botanic Gardens in Jamaica, began the Durban Botanic Garden in 1851. Soon, 10 hectares were increased to 20. McKen began to establish a serious garden of plants of economic value: sugarcane, cinchona (whose bark includes quinine, an important treatment for malaria) tea, coffee, rubber and pineapples.

The spirits of long-gone botanists and plant hunters mingle in the modern gardens. As of old, the oriole, goshawk, paradise flycatcher and Natal robin look on. Today, 150 years later, the Durban Botanic Garden retains the vigour and the enthusiasm of those pioneers who rode out from the Royal Hotel to found Durban's brightest jewel.

Don't miss …

» … these gardens, which are now just a short walk from the country's largest medicinal plant markets, the Warwick triangle. The gardens feature an enviable collection of subtropical trees, palms and orchids.

» … the rarest cycad in the world, *Encephalartos woodii*.

» … the orchid house.

Best time to visit

Spring, autumn: The orchids are at their best

Garden details

70 St Thomas Rd, Durban
Open 16 Apr–15 Sept, 7.30am–5.15pm; 16 Sept–15 Apr, 7.30am–5.45pm
Tel +27 (0)31 201130
www.durbanbotanicgardens.org.za
Size 145 hectares

Left: The Mind and Mood Garden is a feast for the senses.
Above: The sunken garden.

79. Kirstenbosch National Botanic Garden

A visit to Kirstenbosch is a step back in time to reveal the unique history, botany and the best example of the native Fynbos flora and fauna. The Fynbos Biome is made up of 8700 species, most confined to the Cape area and many under grave threat of extinction.

Timeline 1895, developed 1913

Description

Set against the eastern slopes of Table Mountain, this garden has spectacular views. Walkers will love the strenuous walk to the top along Smuts Track. Those who prefer gentler style of garden tour can recline on one of the rolling lawns with a picnic.

In 1895, Cecil John Rhodes bought this property and when he died in 1902 he bequeathed it to the people of South Africa. In 1913, Henry Pearson, a botanist from Cambridge University, took a massive pay cut to develop the site as a botanic garden. Today, it is a proud showcase of South African flora.

Because of the challenging topography, a great deal of construction was needed. For the first 50 years most of the stonework was manually done, usually with trolleys, mules, carts and crawlers. Local Table Mountain stone has been used and today you can see cobbling, curbing, dry stone walls, rockeries and stone features, which are a large part of the landscape.

Left: Mathews' Rockery displays succulents and bulbs from the dry parts of South Africa and annual daisies from the dry Namaqualand region put on a spectacular show of colour during late winter and spring (August-October).
Above right: Vygies or ice-plants transform into a kaleidoscope of colour in late spring (October)–brilliant pinks, purple, magenta, yellow and white.
Below right: The King Protea, Protea cynaroides, is South Africa's national flower and has the largest flower head of all the proteas, with some flower heads reaching up to 30cm in diameter.
Next page left: Kirstenbosch's main lawn with red flowering aloes with oak tree in winter.
Next page right: The pincushion bush, Leucospermum cordifolium.

Don't miss …

» … Camphor Avenue, which is permanently shaded by camphor trees (*Cinnamomum camphora*) from China and Japan that were planted by Cecil John Rhodes more than a century ago along an avenue that led to his Cecilia Estate, south of Kirstenbosch. Shade-loving plants such as plectranthus, haemanthus, crinum, clivia and others are grown under the massive, spreading branches.

» … the row of Moreton Bay figs (*Ficus macrophylla*, from Australia), also planted by Rhodes, that now forms the eastern boundary of the main lawns.

Best time to visit

September–October: The most beautiful time to visit when the carpets of spring wildflowers are in flower, cushioning the ground so that the mountain appears to float on a sea of flowers. The whole garden is magic as the rainbow-coloured fields of Namaqualand annuals and spring bulbs burst into flower. Pincushion bush (*Leucospermum*) are in full flower at this time.

Garden details

Rhodes Drive, Newlands, Cape Town

Private Bag X7, Claremont

Open Sep–March, 8am–7pm; Apr–Aug, 8am–6pm; sunset concerts Nov–Apr, 5.30pm

Tel +27 (0)21 799 8899/799 8783

www.sanbi.org/frames/kirstfam

Size 528 hectares, 36 hectares cultivated

Chapter 7

THE PACIFIC

Early European settlers in Australia and New Zealand planted the English gardens with which they were familiar. This tradition has changed over the past 200 years. Garden design in Australia and New Zealand has now been liberated, unfettered by historic traditions. Contemporary gardens demonstrate a shift in focus with plant selection and design influenced more by climatic factors, location and latitude rather that a preconceived idea of what a garden is. The result is an interesting development in dry land gardens, and a love affair with indigenous plants, Mediterranean plants and tropical-style gardens. Australia's isolation has prompted gardeners to read widely and travel for horticultural and design inspiration, so it is not surprising that garden styles are so diverse, inspired from cultures all around the world.

Wychwood looks across to the Western Tiers, Tasmania.

Australia

Australians are known for their innovation and sense of space. They think independently and creatively. Across the continent there are many glorious gardens created in a variety of climates; from the tropics of Brisbane, to the desert garden of Cranbourne, to the cool temperate climate of Wychwood in Tasmania. The gardens in this book have been chosen for their merit and diversity. The gardens are a testament to the determination of their owners to overcome adversity and to strive to create their own ideas of what a garden can be. These gardens open regularly for visitors, many as a part of Australia's Open Garden Scheme.

Rural charm at Red Cow Farm.

80. The Australian Garden, Cranbourne

This new garden showcases the beauty and diversity of Australian plants and landscapes, exploring the connections that exist between landscape, plants and people. It has a deep sense of place and is a living lesson in water conservation. Set within the greater 363 hectares of wetlands and woodlands 50 kilometres from Melbourne in the Royal Botanic Gardens at Cranbourne, this destination is not to be missed.

Timeline: 2006

Description

At a cost of $14.5 million, leading landscape architects Taylor Cullity Lethlean and plant designer Paul Thompson designed the Australian garden as a dynamic series of living and learning landscapes within a much larger wild bushland area. Being lovers of the Australian 'Outback', we enjoy the journey through this garden. Start with the Red Sand Garden, an expanse of Australia's red heartland desert with contrasting grey foliage imitating native, mass plantings of *Acacia binervia* and *Spinifex sericeus* stabilise the sand. The lower slopes are covered with a carpet of emu apple (*Kunzea pomifera*), also called native cranberry, whose fruit has a flavour of spicy apple.

Expect to see abundant wildflowers including Albany daisy, kangaroo-paw, pin-cushion bush, pineapple bush, rope-rush, popflower, snakebush, mat-rush and a large collection of stunning mature 3m high grass trees. Much of this garden is low growing, however the Eucalyptus Walk is the exception. Native tree species and their hybrids such as paperbark (*melaleuca*) and honey-myrtle (*hakea*) demonstrate Australian plants that have adapted to drought and long dry spells.

The Dry River Bed Garden reminds us of the ephemeral nature of water within the Australian landscape and the power of water to shape the land on a seasonal basis. The creek bed in the Rockpool Waterway cleverly comes and goes before your eyes—a thought-provoking technique that mirrors the real Australian climatic cycle. Plants grow in curvilinear bars of sand along the riverbed, reflecting the large river systems that flow beneath the land surface as part of the artesian water supply. There are many lessons here for dry climate gardeners.

Don't miss:

» the Rockpool Waterway, framed by a giant rust-covered steel sculpture depicting mountain ranges and the smooth-barked apple (*Angophora costata*), is under-planted with dwarf lilly pillies and guinea flowers.
» the five Exhibition Gardens, which change regularly and demonstrate design ideas for the use of Australian plants in home gardens.

Best time to visit

August–September: Spring wildflowers

Garden details

Cranbourne, Royal Botanic Gardens Melbourne
Cnr Ballarto Road and Botanic Drive, Cranbourne, Vic (off South Gippsland Highway); Melway
Ref: 133 K10.
Open every day 9am–5pm; Closed Christmas Day and days of total fire ban
Tel +61 (0)3 5990 2200
www.rbg.vic.gov.au/rbg_cranbourne
Size 11 hectares

Left: Sunny paper daisies, Xerochrysum bracteatum 'Dargan Hill Monarch'.
Right: Desert Garden planted with paper daisies.

81. Cloudehill Nursery and Garden

This inspired garden translates the ideas of famous English 'Arts and Crafts' gardens, Hidcote and Sissinghurst, into a beautiful Australian setting. Situated in the heart of the Dandenong Ranges and surrounded by massive mountain ash trees, this garden has developed into one of the best in Australia.

Timeline: 1890, nursery 1930, re-developed 1995

Description

Cloudehill is a day trip from Melbourne, located at the top of the Dandenong Ranges with stunning views over the Yarra Valley to the mountains. Rose-coloured brick walls compartmentalise most of the 20 garden rooms. Formal gardens on the upper terraces dissolve into meadow gardens on the lower slope.

The flower borders of the main terrace are a signature of owner Jeremy Francis and feature perennials flowering throughout summer and autumn. There is great diversity in the garden, with each 'room' crammed full of colour, textural foliages, interplay of light and shadow and styles of topiary. In the Green Theatre eyes can rest and take in a different aesthetic—wedding ceremonies are held here as are classes in Tai Chi, yoga and plein-air painting.

A pair of Japanese maples (*Acer palmatum* 'Dissectum Atropurpureum'), imported from Japan, date from 1928. There are more fine trees in the woodland area with European beech, magnolias, maples, tree peonies and a fine collection of Himalayan tree rhododendrons.

Don't miss:

» any part of the garden, the nursery, the café, the restaurant.

Take a picnic from the café and stay as long as you can.

» two fastigiate ornamental flowering crabapples, *Malus* Ballerina 'Maypole' in spring.

Best time to visit

August: Grape hyacinths, daffodils and magnolias

September: Bluebells and early rhododendrons

October: Japanese tree peonies, lilac and rhodos

November: Late-flowering rhodos

December–March: The perennial borders at their best

April: Grasses and weeping maples colour up

June: Cyclamen

Garden details

89 Olinda-Monbulk Rd, Olinda, Vic 3788

Open daily 9am–5pm

Tel +61 (0)3 9751 1009

www.cloudehill.com.au

Left: The high standard of horticulture in this flower border is a signature of Jeremy Francis.
Above: A little pocket of England in Victoria's Dandenong's.

82. Red Cow Farm

Red Cow Farm enjoys a picturesque rural location near Sutton Forest, approximately 1.5 hours drive from Sydney and Canberra and is named for the red Hereford cows that once roamed over this property. We believe it is developing into one of the finest gardens in Australia. Red Cow Farm has an interesting monastic theme, a superb choice of plantings and a strong appreciation of every season with a clever succession of flowering. All this makes it a perfect destination for a day trip from Sydney.

Timeline: 1994

'It will never be finished. The garden is a canvas, but unlike a painter's, it is never finished, always evolving and, as it ages, micro climates change and present opportunities for greater scope for plant combinations.'

Ali Mentesh, Red Cow Farm

Description

An apparent simplicity disguises a garden of sophisticated structure and ambitious planting schemes. Developed 'room by room' around an historic 1820's farm cottage, the garden didn't develop on paper but rather it was stepped out spatially.

There are 20 garden rooms in all, including the exuberant Cottage Garden, Monastery Garden, Abbess's Garden, a woodland, beech walk, lake, bog garden, orchard and kitchen garden.

Rose lovers will adore the garden as roses grow to perfection here, many partnered with large-flowered clematis that twine through them. Some pillars support three roses and three clematis each colour coded. This is intensive horticulture, the result of a generous feeding and watering schedule.

The seasonal changes in light offer new perspectives in the garden, with autumn's lower and softer light bringing forward a different colour palette to the strong-coloured planting schemes that work so well under the intense light of an Australian summer.

Don't miss …

» … the Monastery Garden, a pseudo-religious experience achieved with plants.

» …. the Abbess's Garden, a stunning collection of rare and unusual perennials, a garden of old-fashioned roses and clematis.

» … the collection of bleeding hearts (*Dicentra spp.*) in early spring.

Left: Grass pathways meander through this expansive garden.
Above: Partially hidden entrance to the Monastery Garden.
Next page left: Religious symbolism unites this garden
Next page right: Clever use of canna foliage complements monkshood and dahlias.

Best time to visit

Spring and autumn

Garden details

Illawarra Highway, Sutton Forest, NSW 2577
Open daily mid Mar–mid May, 10am–4pm
or by appointment
Tel +61 (0)2 4868 1842
Size 2.5 hectares

83. Dennis Hundscheidt's Garden

Dennis Hundscheidt is both a master garden designer and a subtropical plantsperson and he has transformed a typical Brisbane suburban block into Australia's best subtropical garden. His interest in collecting plants, especially cordylines and bromeliads from all parts of the tropical world has resulted in a suburban paradise second to none.

Timeline: 2000

Description

This is a normal suburban block but it feels much bigger than it really is due to a few design tricks. It is a tranquil tropical setting, created by a languid stream that moves gently, using the sweet bore water from the site, leading you on a slow journey through the garden. Sweeping green lawn disappears in and out of bold foliages and garden beds are crammed full of exciting plants always harmoniously combined.

All the old favourites are here: fucrea, cordyline, rhoeo and bromeliads but it is the fresh and vibrant arrangements that create such an eye-catching scene. The plant collection is well designed with pavilions, water elements and sculpture punctuating the space. This garden offers style and substance along with impressive horticultural skill.

One hundred palms provide the framework for the garden. The silver-grey Bismarck's palm (*Bismarckia nobilis*) is under-planted with sensational foliages. Bold leaf shapes and exotic tropical flowers, including gingers, hibiscus and dripping heliconias, combine to create a living masterpiece. Subtle and restrained use of Asian sculpture emphasises the tranquil, meditative mood of this garden.

Don't miss …

»   … the tricks: fake vistas that make this garden look bigger than it is, disappearing views and the screened boundary fences.

Left: Crabs Claw, Heliconia, feature in this tropical garden.
Above: The Balinese pavilion is flanked with Mauritius Hemp, Furcraea foetida var mediopicta, and pink flowering mussaenda.
Next page left: Silver leaved palms, Bismarkia nobilis, provide stunning accents. Next page right: The spring-fed stream runs through the garden.

Best time to visit

February: When the garden opens for the Australia's Open Garden Scheme.

Garden details

173 Young St, Sunnybank, Brisbane, Qld 4109
Open Check Australian's Open Garden Scheme for details
Size 1000 square metres
www.opengarden.org.au

84. Wychwood

Karen Hall and Peter Cooper have found their destiny turning empty paddocks on the edge of a running stream in a quiet and beautiful Tasmanian valley into a glorious garden called Wychwood, 50 minutes from where the ferry docks at Davenport or two and a half hours drive from Hobart.

Timeline: 1993

Description

An avenue of elegant silver birch welcomes you to Wychwood, a garden blessed with a fabulous location, backdropped by the Great Western Tiers on one side, Gog Range and Mount Roland on the other. The garden opens out as you pass the nursery and the garage and grassy green paths lead past wide curvaceous beds, which are intensely planted.

It's all soft and artistic with grasses swaying in the breeze and soft colours melting into each other. Everything is meticulously planned to look effortlessly natural and uncontrived. The secret to how well the plants grow is the soil – it looks good enough to eat! No fertilisers are used here, the soil nutrient comes from near edible compost, which is spread over the beds in winter once plants are pruned back.

Espaliered apples and plums are a signature of Wychwood. Every wall and fence has one, even the low perimeter fence around the potager has the famous heritage 'Cat's Head' apple. They bring a fun element and make good use of north and west-facing walls and fences. The children's cubby, built by Peter, with vertical boards and high-pitched roofs harking back to his Scandinavian roots, gives the garden a picturesque backdrop.

Don't miss …

» … the garden studio with craft items and home-cooked jams and jellies for sale. For a meditative experience, you must walk the medieval grass labryrinth, a 'seven ring unicursal labryrinth' – a design dating back to 3000 years BC, which has been adapted for the Wychwood logo.

» … the orchard, featuring 25 varieties of heirloom apples.

» … the specialist nursery with frost and heat-proof plants.

Left: Soft and romantic ornamental grasses give autumn interest.
Above and next page: Meticulous planting schemes make this garden look natural and uncontrived.
Page 258: Vegetable garden is bountiful as well as beautiful.
Page 259: Spiral hedge is kept well trimmed and graduated in height.

Best time to visit

Late spring, summer and autumn to see the perennials and ornamental grasses

Garden details

80 Den Road, Mole Creek, Tas 7304
Open Thur–Sat, 10am–5pm; Sept–end of May; closed Jun, Jul, Aug
Tel +61 (0)3 6363 1210
www.wychwoodtasmania.com
Size 1 hectare

85. Ian Potter Children's Garden, Melbourne Royal Botanic Gardens

This new garden in the centre of Melbourne, is cleverly designed for children: for exploration, discovery, education, interaction, play and, best of all, fun. It's a place where little minds will grow. This is no collection of slippery dips and roundabouts. Instead, carefully designed structures, water features, climbing statues, plants and gardens intrigue, teach and excite children in a safe environment.

Timeline: 2004

Description

Giant, wrought-iron gates open into the Meeting Place where bench seating and the five giant Queensland bottle trees (*Brachychiton rupestris*) indicate you have arrived somewhere special.

Nearby are the impressive sculptural forms of 2.5-metre vertical basalt rocks and twisted snow gums (*Eucalyptus pauciflora*). Exploring further you find the Ruin Garden, a lost world with rocky grotto, stone arches and ramparts covered in lush rainforest vines and trees. The giant leaves of gunnera fascinate and the ancient trunks of river red gum (*Eucalyptus camaldulensis*) challenge youngsters to climb.

There is plenty of sensual inspiration. A sand pit provides opportunities to dig. Building cubbies from 'jungle' vegetation is encouraged. An artificial mist fills the gullies and hollows and turns this into a magical place. It's a treat to watch children playing creatively and excitedly with, and among, plants in a garden.

Don't miss …

» … the Kitchen Garden with exciting and interactive vegetables, fruit trees, herbs, flowers and with compost bins.
» … the chance to grow your own plants in the Potting Shed.
» … the Bamboo Forest jungle for a great game of hide-and-seek.

Best time to visit

Any day of the year

Garden details

Birdwood Ave, South Yarra, Vic 3141

Open Wed–Sun, 10am–4pm; daily 10am–4pm during Victorian state-school holidays; closed Jul–Aug (at the end of the Victorian July school holidays); closed Christmas Day, Boxing Day, New Year's Day and Good Friday

Tel +61 (0)3 9252 2300

www.rbg.vic.gov.au/rbg_melbourne/ian_potter_foundation_childrens_garden

Left: The Gorge is a metaphorical forest with tall rocks and twisted weeping snow gums.
Above right: The Children's Kitchen Garden is interactive, for lessons in gardening.
Below right: The Magic Pudding characters—just for kids!

New Zealand

New Zealand's cool and moist climate sustains some of the most wonderful gardens in the world. New Zealanders love their gardens and thousands are opened regularly to visitors. New Zealand's particular geography means that no garden is far from the sea so an extraordinarily wide range of plants grow well in a moist temperate environment. Gardens styles are just as diverse: some are English style with herbaceous borders; others offer a fresh innovative approach using native plants. We time our garden tours to include the Taranaki Rhododendron Festival, the Ellerslie Flower Show and the new Auckland Garden Show.

Indian Char Bagh Garden at Hamilton Gardens with Flanders poppies.

86. Ayrlies

Ayrlies is situated in gently rolling country east of Auckland city and is one of New Zealand's best-known gardens, with twelve acres sculpted from bare paddock by owner Beverley McConnell. Ayrlies is planted for overall visual effect although each area has its own special character.

Timeline: 1964

Description

The entrance to the garden is dramatic, down a series of steps past a giant, noisy watery cascade. The garden opens out before you with a vivid green lawn sweeping down to the lake at the bottom. Now the scene is calm. Walk along the water's edge past grasses and ferns that soften the waterways and accentuate the tranquillity. We love the easy natural look of this garden and yet the design has been carefully contrived. Stop in the waterside pavilion, which was covered in flowering clematis at the time of our visit, for magic views across the lake to the garden beyond.

There are four waterfalls and three large ponds planted with waterlilies, irises, bog plants and primulas. It's a gentle stroll through the garden, like walking into a painted canvas.

As you walk back uphill towards the house you will see the Lurid Border with its strong but sensitive use of colour that is the hallmark of this garden. Take the steps back down through the rose garden where romantic old garden roses are planted with clematis twining through each one and foxgloves and aquilegias join them in flower. You will catch glimpses of the waters of Hauraki Gulf. A fabulous wetland links the garden to the sea.

Don't miss …

»   … the wildflower meadow at its peak in
    December.
»   … a peep over the picket fence into the
    garden cottage with its own garden of roses,
    delphiniums, dianthus and iris … dreamy!

Best time to visit

The challenge has been to have some plant or
vista at its best every week of the year. Spring is
a wonderful season when roses and clematis flower
in unison.

Garden details

Ayrlies, 125 Potts Rd, R.D.1, Howick 2014
Tel +64 (0)9 530 8706
Open by appointment only
Size 5 hectares
www.ayrlies.co.nz

Left: Clematis is a favourite of Beverley McConnell.
Above: The Lurid Border with strong but sensitive use of colour.
*Next page left: The woodland garden, with arum lily, leading to
the pond.*
*Next page right: Arum, candelabra primula and the 'knees' of
the swamp cypress.*

87. Hamilton Gardens

Two hours drive south of Auckland lies Hamilton and one of New Zealand's premier tourist destinations, Hamilton Gardens. Developed on a waste dump, it is now an impressive collection of gardens designed to tell the 'story of gardens'.

Timeline 1960, development 1982

Description

This garden is a bit like a horticultural theme park with a lot to digest in a small space. Allow yourself plenty of time for this visit and don't linger in any one area if it doesn't grab you; there's something else just around the corner. First is the Paradise Garden Collection with gardens representing significant design traditions, including the Chinese Scholars Garden, English Flower Garden, Japanese Garden of Contemplation, American Modernist Garden, Italian Renaissance Gardens and Indian Char Bagh Garden. There is also a Productive Garden Collection, a Cultivar Garden Collection and a Landscape Garden Collection with areas representing different historic interpretations of an idealised landscape.

Our favourite part is the 'Persian carpet' effect in the Indian Char Bagh Garden, where the sunken beds allow the flowers to bloom at the same height as the path in a blaze of colour. If you time your visit for late in the day, the scent lingers, trapped by the high walls. We also love the organic gardening concept in the Kitchen Garden where you can learn all about permaculture and sustainable living.

Allow time for the Rose Garden and take notes of your favourites. We particularly love the French roses for their fragrance and old-fashioned, full-petalled blooms. With 4200 roses comprising approximately 230 cultivars, this is one of the largest rose gardens in

New Zealand. Hamilton is a good place to learn about the native flora of New Zealand and to get your eye in for what you will see growing wild when tramping through the country. You can also catch up with some fabulous new varieties such as the handsome silver-foliaged Renga Renga lily (*Arthropodium*).

Don't miss …

» … the Indian Char Bagh Garden, a 'Riverside Garden' with a plan very similar to that at the Taj Mahal, but on a very much smaller scale.

Best time to visit

September–October: For the rhododendrons and their exquisite fragrance in the early evening

December: Peak flowering for the 'Persian carpet' in the Indian Char Bagh Garden

Garden details

Cobham Drive (State Highway 1) at the southern end of Hamilton city

Open 7.30am–5.30pm in winter and to 8pm in summer

Tel 64 (0)7 838 6782

www.hamiltongarden.co.nz

Size 58 hectares

Left: The rose garden. Above right: Picnic by the lake.
Below right: The Indian Char Bagh garden.
Next page left: The Italianate Renaissance inspired garden.
Next page right: The view from the Chinese garden.

First published in Australia in 2009 by
New Holland Publishers (Australia) Pty Ltd
Sydney • Auckland • London • Cape Town

1/66 Gibbes Street Chatswood NSW 2067 Australia
218 Lake Road Northcote Auckland New Zealand
86 Edgware Road London W2 2EA United Kingdom
80 McKenzie Street Cape Town 8001 South Africa

A record of this book is held at the National Library of Australia

ISBN 9781877069512

Publisher: Fiona Schultz
Publishing Manager: Lliane Clarke
Senior Project Editor: Joanna Tovia
Designer: Tania Gomes and Natasha Hayles
Production Manager: Olga Dementiev
Printer: SNP/Leefung Printing Co. (China)

10 9 8 7 6 5 4 3 2 1

Photo credits
We'd like to thank the following gardens, photographers and photo libraries for contributing the following images:

Front Cover: Villa Ephrussi de Rothschild, Courtesy Photolibrary
Back Cover: Keukenhof, Courtesy Keukenhof

Pg 12 Photolibrary, Pg 22/23 Peter Whitehead, Pg 26 Japan Tourism, Pg 30/31 Photolibrary, Pg 34 Photolibrary, Pg 36 Photolibrary, Pg 40 Garden World Images, Pg 48 Garden World Images, Pg 50/51 Photolibrary, Pg 56/57 Garden World Images, Pg 58 Garden World Images, Pg 62/63 Photolibrary, Pg 64/65 Photolibrary, pg 74/75 Garden World Images, Pg 76/77 Heligan Gardens, Pg 82 Location Photography, Pg 84/85 Photolibrary, Pg 86/87 Jim Henderson, pg 88 Brian Chapple Pg 89 David Robertson, pg 94/95 Photolibrary, Pg 98 courtesy Keukenhof, Pg 122-125 Photolibrary, Pg 128/129 Photolibrary, pg 132 Photolibrary, Pg 136/137 Garden World Images, Pg 138 courtesy Keukenhof, Pg 141 Photolibrary, Pg 146-149 courtesy Keukenhof, Pg 150/151 Photolibrary, Pg 158 Photolibrary, Pg 161 top Photolibrary, Pg 162/163 Photolibrary, Pg 164/165 Photolibrary, Pg 171 Photolibrary, Pg 186 Garden World Images, Pg 196 courtesy Butchart Gardens, Pg 198/199 courtesy Butchart Gardens, Pg 204 courtesy Longwood Gardens, Pg 206-207 courtesy Longwood Gardens, Pg 214 Photolibrary, Pg 218 courtesy of Mount Vernon Ladies Association, Pg 222 Alice Notten, SANBI, Kirstenbosch National Botanic Garden, Pg 224 Photolibrary, Pg 226-227 Photolibrary, Pg 228/229 Photolibrary, Pg 230 Alice Notten, Pg 232/234 Alice Notten, Pg 234 Adam Harrower, SANBI, Pg 235 Alice Notten, SANBI, Pg 238 Peter Cooper, courtesy Wychwood. Pg 242/243 Janusz Molinski, courtesy Royal Botanic Gardens Melbourne. Pg 244/245 Claire Takus, courtesy Cloudehill, Pg 250-253 Glenn Weiss, Pg 254-259 Peter Cooper, Pg 262 Courtesy Hamilton Gardens, Pg 265-267 Courtesy Ayrlies, Pg 268-271 Courtesy Hamilton Gardens.